JOSSEY-BASS GUIDES
TO ONLINE TEACHING AND LEARNING

Continuing to Engage the Online Learner

Activities and Resources for Creative Instruction

Rita-Marie Conrad

J. Ana Donaldson

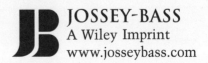

JOSSEY-BASS
A Wiley Imprint
www.josseybass.com

Published by Jossey-Bass

A Wiley Imprint

One Montgomery Street, Suite 1200, San Francisco, CA 94104-4594—www.josseybass.com

Jossey-Bass books and products are available through most bookstores. To contact Jossey-Bass directly call our Customer Care Department within the U.S. at 800-956-7739, outside the U.S. at 317-572-3986, or fax 317-572-4002.

Wiley publishes in a variety of print and electronic formats and by print-on-demand. Some material included with standard print versions of this book may not be included in e-books or in print-on-demand. If this book refers to media such as a CD or DVD that is not included in the version you purchased, you may download this material at **http://booksupport.wiley.com**. For more information about Wiley products, visit **www.wiley.com**.

Library of Congress Cataloging-in-Publication Data
Conrad, Rita-Marie.
   Continuing to engage the online learner : activities and resources for creative instruction /
Rita-Marie Conrad, J. Ana Donaldson. – First edition.
       pages cm. – (Jossey-Bass guides to online teaching and learning ; 35)
    Includes bibliographical references and index.
   ISBN 978-1-118-00017-5 (pbk.), ISBN 978-1-118-26025-8 (ebk.), ISBN 978-1-118-23544-7 (ebk.),
ISBN 978-1-118-22167-9 (ebk.)
   1. Internet in education. 2. Computer-assisted instruction. I. Donaldson, J. Ana. II. Title.
   LB1044.87.C655 2012
   371.33'44678–dc23

                         2012012679

Printed in the United States of America
FIRST EDITION
PB Printing   10 9 8 7 6 5 4 3 2 1

Contents

Tables, Figure, and Exhibit

TABLES

FIGURE

EXHIBIT

To Larry and Al
For their loving support

Preface

Online learning has grown rapidly since our prior book, *Engaging the Online Learner,* was first published in 2004. Numerous books and research studies on the topic are now available, which may be one indicator that educators in both online and blended learning environments continue to strive to create more effective learning experiences for their students and see interaction as key to that effectiveness.

Educators are continuing to ask themselves how they can bring to life the names of the learners they read in their course sites and how to design a learning experience that goes beyond mere content presentation to being transformative both in learners' lives and in the world as well.

Why have we chosen to write another book on engagement? As online educators ourselves, we have continued to reflect on how we can energize a learning environment and empower learners to adopt responsibility for their own learning without extensive verbal or physical communication cues. We have watched the rise of social networking and the new philosophy of connectivism that focuses on personal learning networks used by each learner. As a result, our Phases of Engagement model has evolved. The framework continues to provide a means for instructors to guide learners in the development of skills needed to engage with the content and with one another online without the instructor being the primary initiator of knowledge generation and interaction. However, the new fifth phase of engagement, called Continue, looks beyond the course experience and discusses how the engaged learning experience will influence future learning experiences and career development. This book has also been influenced by our work with fellow online faculty who have expressed a continued desire for new ideas to enhance their online instruction.

As with our first book, the activity examples provided by experienced online instructors across the nation continue to be the strength of this book. The activities provide numerous ways in which each phase of engaged learning can be implemented in an online environment.

We have updated our thoughts behind the theory of engaged learning. While that was done very basically in *Engaging the Online Learner,* this book focuses on additional aspects such as social networks and the philosophy of connectivism, which have gathered momentum and are affecting online learning in ways not foreseen a decade ago.

The intended audience of the book is online educators, whether they be in K–12, higher education, or corporate environments, who may be new to the online learning environment or who are dealing with learners who are relatively new to online collaboration. It is our hope that this book will also be helpful to experienced online practitioners who are seeking to improve their established online courses, as well as instructional designers who are developing online courses.

OVERVIEW OF THE CONTENTS

The book contains two parts. Part One discusses foundational aspects of online engagement. Chapter 1 discusses the foundation of past theory and the latest issues that are shaping online engagement, as well as the role of the learner and instructor. Chapter 2 contains the updated Phases of Engagement model introduced in our earlier work *Engaging the Online Learner.* Chapter 3 focuses on unique aspects to consider when implementing the Phases of Engagement model. Chapter 4 discusses key elements needed to effectively assess online engaged learning.

Part Two, which consists of Chapters 5 through 9, presents activities for each of the five Phases of Engagement. Chapter 5 discusses Phase 1, Connect, activities;

Chapter 6 contains Phase 2, Communicate, activities; Chapter 7 provides Phase 3, Collaborate, activities; and Chapter 8 focuses on Phase 4, Co-Facilitate, types of activities. In Chapter 9 activities for the new Phase of Engagement, Phase 5, Continuation, are presented. Activities can be used as they appear or can be adapted to your particular content. Each activity contains the title and the name of the instructor who tested the activity in an online environment and submitted it for inclusion in the book.

ACKNOWLEDGMENTS

As with our first book, *Engaging the Online Learner,* this book is built on instructional activities from colleagues across the nation who have focused on creating an engaging learning experience for their students. We are indebted to faculty members who shared their activities for inclusion in this book. This has again been a community endeavor, and we are humbled by their collegiality in this endeavor.

In addition, this book would not have happened without Bill Draves and the Learning Resources Network (LERN), who facilitated our ability to reach faculty across the United States. We are also grateful to Rena Palloff and Keith Pratt, Rosemary Lehman and Simone Conceicao, who continue to inspire us with their work, which strives to better the online learning experience for faculty and students. Our gratitude also goes to Judith Boettcher and Sharon Smaldino for their mentorship, and to the director and staff of the Annual Conference on Distance Teaching and Learning in Madison, Wisconsin, who provided the environment in which the first *Engaging the Online Learner* book was conceived and in which this current book was nurtured. Our deep appreciation also goes to our very understanding and patient editors at Jossey-Bass, Alison Knowles, Erin Null, and Justin Frahm.

We hope you will let us know how you use the activities in this book!

Rita-Marie Conrad
Durham, North Carolina
ritamarie.conrad@duke.edu
J. Ana Donaldson
Cedar Falls, Iowa
ana.donaldson@cfu.net

The Authors

Rita-Marie Conrad is the instructional strategist and technologist for Duke University's Institute for Educational Excellence in the School of Nursing, where she assists in establishing instructional guidelines and helps faculty in utilizing the most effective instructional strategies and technologies. She spent over a decade at Florida State University, where she assisted in the development and leadership of two online programs: the instructional systems major in Performance Improvement and Human Resource Development, and the instructional systems major in Open and Distance Learning. She has designed and taught online courses on topics such as online collaboration, learning theories, designing online instruction, and developing e-learning strategies for training programs for institutions such as Florida State University, Fielding Graduate University, Walden University, Nova Southeastern University, and Capella University. Conrad has consulted on the design and implementation of online learning courses, evaluated online programs, and provided educational technology consulting and training to K–12 teachers and higher education faculty. She interacts with hundreds of faculty as an online instructor for courses such as Designing Online Instruction, sponsored by the Learning Resources Network (LERN). She has presented at conferences sponsored by the International Council for Distance Education (ICDE), the University of Wisconsin, the Minnesota State Colleges and Universities, the League of Innovation, and the Association for Educational Communication and Technology (AECT) on a variety of online learning topics. Conrad coauthored two books with Judith Boettcher: *Faculty Guide for Moving Teaching and Learning to the Web* (League for Innovation in the Community College, 1999, 2004) and *The Online Teaching Survival Guide: Simple and Practical Pedagogical Tips* (Jossey-Bass, 2010). She wrote *Engaging the Online Learner* (Jossey-Bass, 2004, 2011) with J. Ana Donaldson, as well as *Assessing Learners Online* (Prentice Hall, 2008) with Albert Oosterhof and Donald Ely. Dr. Conrad holds a Ph.D. in instructional systems from Florida State University and a master's degree in educational media and computers from Arizona State University.

J. Ana Donaldson is an online educator and consultant. She is currently a contributing faculty member for Walden University in their online Ph.D. Educational Technology program. She retired in 2009 as an associate professor of instructional technology from the University of Northern Iowa. Besides her years of classroom experience in creating web-supported learning environments, she is a published author, keynote speaker, and international presenter. She is coauthor with Rita-Marie Conrad of *Engaging the Online Learner* (Jossey-Bass, 2004, 2011). Her publishing credits include a chapter coauthored with Sharon Smaldino and Mary Herring titled "Professional Ethics: Rules Applied to Practice" in the book *Trends and Issues in Instruction Design and Technology* (3rd ed., R. R. Reiser and J. V. Dempsey, Eds.). Donaldson also coauthored the "Managing" chapter with Sharon Smaldino and P. Pearson in the book *Educational Technology: An Analysis and Explanation of the Concept Field Definition* (Al Januszewski, Ed.). Donaldson is the AECT (Association for Educational Communications and Technology) president for 2011–2012. She received a master's degree in instructional technology from Northern Illinois University and holds an Ed.D. in instructional technology, also from Northern Illinois University.

Revisiting Online Engagement

This section of the book presents the theoretical basis for engagement and discusses the latest issues that are shaping online engagement. In addition, the Phases of Engagement model introduced in our earlier work, *Engaging the Online Learner*, is updated and reviewed, along with aspects to consider when implementing the Phases of Engagement model and assessing online engaged learning.

The State of Online Engagement

We must bring 21st-century technology into learning in meaningful ways to engage, motivate, and inspire learners of all ages to achieve.

National Education Technology Plan, 2010

A significant element in meeting the instructional needs of the twenty-first-century learner is to discover effective ways to reach the individual in the context of diverse technology-enhanced opportunities. Since *Engaging the Online Learner* was first published in the early 2000s, the focus on engagement has intensified, as indicated by the numerous publication of books on the topic since that time (Aldrich, 2009; Barkley, 2010; Bonk & Zhang, 2008; Palloff & Pratt, 2005, 2007; Shank, 2007; Watkins, 2005; West & West, 2009). As the emphasis on online learning intensifies, the demand for quality instruction increases. We believe that an awareness of this evolving instructional approach has been captured within the concept of transformational learning. As Merriam, Caffarella, and Baumgartner state, "transformative or transformational (terms used interchangeably in the literature) learning is about change—dramatic, fundamental change in the way we see ourselves and the world in which we live" (2007, p. 130). Additional opportunities need to be provided for online learners and instructors to engage not only with the content, but with one another in the spirit of transformational learning (Mezirow & Associates, 2000). The historical foundations of engagement began with Dewey and continue to evolve with the addition of transformational learning.

FOUNDATIONS OF ENGAGEMENT

The paradigm shift to the instructor as a facilitator of active student learning began with Dewey over a century ago. Dewey (1916/1997) valued teachers' and students' contributions to the learning experience in addition to contributions from diverse and meaningful peer collaboration. Houle's early work in the 1960s identified three adult orientations toward learning. He identified learners as being goal-oriented, activity-oriented, or learning-oriented (Houle, 1988). Malcolm Knowles' (1980) research on adult learners—*andragogy* was his preferred term—determined that an active collaborative learning situation, where the student is self-directed and shares her or his own personal experiences, is one of the key elements to a successful learning experience. Adult learning theory has built heavily on the instructional methodology that is often identified as situational cognition or constructivism. "Concepts such as cognitive apprenticeship, situated learning, reflective practice, and communities of practice are found in both adult learning and constructivist literature" (Merriam, Caffarella, & Baumgartner, 2007, p. 293). Additional theorists have influenced instructional approaches that support adult learners in a learner-focused learning environment.

Bruner, Vygotsky, and Piaget are several of the past theorists who supported the concept that learning is enriched when it includes collaborative and learner-engaged instructional approaches. Bruner wrote that learning includes a "deep human need to respond to others and to operate jointly with them toward an objective" (Bruner, 1966, p. 67). Vygotsky's research introduced the concept of the zone of proximal development (ZPD) (Vygotsky, 1978). The concept of ZPD enforces his belief that individual learning can be expanded with assistance and interaction with a more knowledgeable individual. Piaget (1969), who preferred the term *constructivism* over the term *engaged learning,* conducted further research on Vygotsky's ZPD concept of mentoring-learning relationships. His research findings indicated that the synergy between equal partners results in a richer learning experience because it is not adversely affected by power conflicts. The world of online learning continues to evolve rapidly, with an increasing emphasis on collaborative learning and student engagement.

The concept of the instructor as a *guide on the side* is now being revised even further, with the teacher serving as an additional resource within the expanding learning network that is available through the instant access technology provides to information. Building upon this user-driven access to information, the recent decade saw the introduction of the concept of *connectivism.* George Siemens and Stephen Downs are two of the leading advocates of this emerging view. "Connectivism is a theory describing how learning happens in a digital age . . . The connections that enable us to learn more are more important than our current state of knowing . . . Learning and knowing are constant, ongoing processes (not end states or products)" (Siemens, 2006, pp. 42–43). Viewing knowledge acquisition as a cyclical, ongoing process reinforces our understanding of the ways in which collaborative and transformative learning environments are increasing the richness of the online environment. Connectivism supports the idea that online learning is not limited to a one-way linear path from instructor to student. "The learning process is cyclical, in that learners will connect to a network to share and find new information, will modify their beliefs on the basis of new learning, and will then connect to a network to share these realizations and find new information once more" (Kop & Hill, 2008, p. 1). Siemens recommends a new instructional approach, noting that "advocates of problem-based, discovery and cooperative approaches to learning suggest traditional lecture-based learning is ineffective" (2008, p. 12). Siemens (2008) and Bonk (2007) share the educator's view of the instructor in dual roles: knowledge expert and guide facilitating learner discovery. An online course allows the instructor's role as learning facilitator to enrich the experience for all participants.

ENGAGEMENT IN TODAY'S ONLINE LEARNING ENVIRONMENT

No longer is the learner a passive recipient of wisdom disseminated from the *all-knowing* instructor. Today's online student is expected to be an active participant in her or his own learning experiences. "Many online teachers have observed . . . how online classroom behavior mirrors the shift of power from teacher to student" (Coombs, 2010, p. 24). While it may still be a surprise to some learners to find that online learning requires more from them than some of their earlier classroom and online learning experiences, the message is being more consistently sent by online programs and instructors in the form of student orientations and course guidelines concerning the learner involvement.

The process of online engagement includes the interactions between a teacher and students and also *among* the students within a course's learning community. A great deal of emphasis has been placed on learner engagement, but effective learner engagement is dependent on active participation from each contributor: teacher *and* student. For the learner, "motivation and active learning work together synergistically, and as they interact, they contribute incrementally to increase engagement" (Barkley, 2010, p. 7). The online instructor must remember that "in this century, the first role of the teacher is to maintain and foster enthusiasm for learning. The second role of the teacher is to assist the student in her or his learning and knowledge" (Draves & Coates, 2011, p. 39). Instructor enthusiasm and support are important elements for successful learning experiences.

The focus on instructor engagement is also increasing. Research has shown that a successful online experience is dependent on the interactions between faculty and students (Cavanaugh, 2009). Student engagement has long been considered a foundational element for a successful learning event. However, faculty modeling of dynamic interactions as an instructional strategy is a critical aspect of instructor-to-learner engagement. An important consideration for ensuring course success is a high level of communication opportunities between students and instructor. "Research and experience tell us that prompt feedback is important in online learning settings, where students lack many of the traditional nonverbal cues to which they are accustomed in face-to-face venues" (Finkelstein, 2006, p. 23). The requisites for an effective online instructor are being redefined. Best practices for online teaching have emerged from various authors and organizations in the last few years and signal that instructional roles are shifting from content experts to pedagogical experts addressing student learning within a challenging technology-enriched online context.

Technology continues to be a double-edged sword for engagement. On the one hand, it is the element that enables engagement to occur online. On the other hand, students need to be provided with additional support to overcome unique online barriers usually related to the technology. Many times this needed support needs to come from sources other than the instructor, such as a help desk or classmates willing to be of assistance. Often technical problems are short-lived. Within the first weeks of class, most challenges are resolved by acclimating the students to the course's navigational or posting requirements through specifically assigned simple tasks. When the problems become more long term, then the technology creates "learning distractions" and learning is adversely affected (Lehman & Conceicao, 2010, p. 29). The important lesson to remember is that online learning, as well as learner engagement, is about the *learning* and not the technology. The challenges of dealing with technology cannot be ignored, but technology needs to be secondary to the learning tasks, the learners, motivational considerations, and communication (Smith, 2008). Additional concepts such as social networking and connectivism are also influencing student learning and engagement in today's twenty-first-century classroom.

IMPACT OF SOCIAL NETWORKING AND CONNECTIVISM

The increasing presence of social networking has caused educators to question how today's students learn and communicate newly acquired knowledge. Responses to the impact of twenty-first-century technology on learning resulted in the development of the concept of connectivism discussed earlier. Siemens advocates that learning experiences go beyond the formal classroom: "We live as an integrated experience—we see, know, and function in connections. Life, like knowing, is not an isolated activity—it is a rich, interconnected part of who we are" (2008, p. 16). The collaborative learning experience—the foundation of the Phases of Engagement introduced in our earlier book *Engaging the Online Learner* (Conrad & Donaldson, 2004, 2011)—is built upon the belief that learning is an interactive learning community event. "In connectivism, the starting point for learning occurs when knowledge is actuated through the process of a learner connecting to and feeding information into a learning community" (Kop & Hill, 2008, p. 1). Another result of this learner-focused environment is the growing importance of transformational learning.

INCREASING TRANSFORMATIONAL LEARNING

The beneficial aspects of engagement go beyond reported levels of student satisfaction or performance improvement. A deeper gain is realized in what is termed *transformative* or *transformational learning,* and "the mental construction of experience, inner meaning, and reflection are common components of this approach" (Merriam, Caffarella, & Baumgartner, 2007, p. 130). Student reflection has long been a process within a constructivist-type approach, but this concept refers to how the learning experience has changed (or transformed) the learner.

Building an active and engaging online learning community requires time and attention, just as a gardener must tend to her or his spring flowerbeds. As one of our students has observed, the instructor is planting seeds in the learning community that in the proper conditions will take hold and blossom, hopefully within a time frame that the instructor and students can celebrate.

Today's student is being asked to become an agent for change. Learners might be asked how an experience or newly developed knowledge will make a difference in the way in which they go about their lives. According to Cercone, "adults need to self-reflect on the learning process and be given support for transformational learning" (2008, p. 159). Asking students to document the changes they see in themselves as learners enforces the importance of reflection. To foster transformational learning, the instructional process should include activities that encourage numerous opportunities for self-reflection on the student's experience, including ways in which a learner has been transformed through engagement.

The addition of the online transformative learning component has been of significant importance to us and prompted us to expand our model to include it. We have come to the realization that one of the benefits of an effective collaborative experience is that both the student and the instructor apply the lessons learned about themselves as learners beyond the restrictions of the instructional setting. The reflective portion of the experiences is elevated to the next level of application by what can be transferred beyond the classroom experience. This *transfer* phase is what moves instructors and learners beyond the actual course to an elevated level of engagement and shapes them as they continue to learn throughout their lives.

THE TWENTY-FIRST-CENTURY LEARNER

Practitioners of instructional design and online learning need to understand the evolving characteristics of learners. The online classroom is populated by a high number of nontraditional adult learners, many of whom are trying to balance the demands of their education with the daily needs of family and, often, a career. However, an increasing amount of online learning occurs in the K–12 educational arena, as well as in professional training venues and in blended learning environments. The term *blended* describes educational settings that include both an online and a face-to-face component. The range of online learning styles is expanding. Smith believes it is important to be aware of online students' diverse learning styles: "we need to strive to present information in ways that are useful to all learning styles" (2008, p. 9). Too often instructors teach in ways that demonstrate a dominant or preferred learning style. Today's learner needs not only "anytime, anyplace" learning, but "any way" of learning as well.

The identification of learner traits and motivational foundations is just as critical as determining achievable instructional objectives. Instructors need to understand that adult learners come to the online experience with three separate learning orientations: there are goal-oriented learners who use education as a means of achieving some other goal; activity-oriented learners, who participate for the sake of the activity itself and the social interaction; and learning-oriented participants, who seek knowledge for its own sake" (Merriam, Caffarella, & Baumgartner, 2007, p. 64). Students also come to the online experience with varying degrees of commitment and self-direction.

In addition, we must be aware that technology has shaped student learning styles and preferences: "for today's students, the classroom is the world, and the information students have available at the flip of a switch is infinite" (Coates, 2007, p. 55). How can one instructor satisfy all the needs of the twenty-first-century learner he or she may encounter in the online learning environment? One answer is through being present and open to knowing your learners.

THE ENGAGED EDUCATOR

Engagement of learners begins with an *engaged instructor* and *reflective teacher* (Brookfield, 1995). It is through educator modeling and guidance that a learner is provided a blueprint for becoming a lifelong learner. As Draves and Coates (2011) remind us, "even with the incorporation of the Internet in instruction and education, the teacher becomes more important to a student's learning, not less important, in this century" (p. 37). They go on to state that it is clear that "more of the teacher's time has to be spent in interaction with the students" (p. 39). To be successful in an online environment, the instructor's skill set needs to be broadened.

Instructor engagement depends on a variety of variables, including timely communication and effective time management skills, both of which are discussed in Chapter 3 in the section on managing engagement. However, instructor engagement must begin with a revised personal definition of the instructor's role and teaching philosophy and the creation of an encouraging virtual presence.

INSTRUCTOR'S ROLE AND PHILOSOPHY

The traditional view of the educator as the *sage on the stage* has been replaced by the dual terms of *knowledge expert* and *guide facilitating learner discovery* (Siemens, 2008), as lecture-based delivery approaches prove to have a limited value in the online arena (Siemens, 2008). Another term that has gained acceptance is that of *learning concierge* (Bonk, 2007). A hotel concierge is accountable for increasing the value of your experience as a guest. This valued professional is trained to direct you to quality experiences and be of assistance for unforeseen contingencies. In the emerging world of personal learning connections, the online instructor no longer is the sole possessor of the content knowledge. Providing additional resources, while challenging and questioning the student, is part of the instructor's redefined responsibilities.

Transformative reflection often plays a role in determining an online instructor's teaching philosophy. Without a front row of students nodding their heads in agreement in response to an instructor's comment, educators benefit from reflecting on their philosophies regarding the important considerations for teaching online and what can be improved in their own instructional methodologies.

The transformational portion of the term occurs when we implement changes in response to needs for improvement. Teaching online is a dynamic process that involves high levels of energetic interaction and quiet moments of contemplation.

CREATING A SENSE OF PRESENCE

The sense of presence in an online course has been identified as a critical component in the interactions between the instructor and the students (Munro, 1998). Lehman and Conceicao define the concept of presence in this way: "It looks and feels as if the instructor is accessible to the learners and that the learners are accessible to the instructor and each other, and that the technology is transparent to the learning process" (2010, p. 3). Creating effective collaborative learning communities and the acquisition of knowledge through dialogue and reflection all necessitate an effective social and cognitive presence: "Although the natural and appropriate inclination is to first direct interaction efforts to establishing social presence and creating interrelationships, this is only a precondition for a purposeful and worthwhile learning experience. Teaching presence is important for the creation and sustainability of a community of inquiry focused on exploration, integration, and testing of concepts and solutions" (Garrison & Cleveland-Innes, 2005, p. 135).

An essential skill for the online instructor is the ability to create a detectable teaching presence in the virtual setting to support a deeper level of interaction and learning than is expected in an online offering. Where online engagement is related to participation and interaction, *presence* has been further defined as "the dynamic interplay of thought, emotion, and behavior" (Lehman & Conceicao, 2010, p. 4). The instructor's creation of a supportive teaching presence is a critical element for successful interaction not only between the instructor and learners, but also among learners themselves.

One way an instructor's course presence becomes evident is by the demonstration of her or his own engagement. A personal element is provided by the inclusion of examples from the instructor's experiences or the inclusion of case studies to further the discussion. Another strategy is to include a welcoming video during the first week of a course. The video can be developed simply with a YouTube level of production to demonstrate a sense of the instructor's engagement and accessibility. A textual way to indicate emotions or to emphasize a statement is to use emoticons. A happy face (☺) is helpful to designate a humorous comment that might be misunderstood without additional visual cues. The use of available multimedia resources is another effective way to support course content or to introduce a new concept. The outcome of an effective instructor presence is a virtual learning environment that encourages inquiry and discussion in a non-threatening setting.

MOBILE TECHNOLOGY

While accommodating the newest technology should not be the primary focus of online learning, its influence cannot be ignored. Seemingly overnight, a variety of portable devices have been born. These devices and their associated software, or "apps," have expanded the possibility for increased instructor and learner engagement and have merged functions that were previously available on separate devices.

There is a growing trend at many universities to offer courses through mobile devices such as smartphones. Research indicates this is also true within K–12 learning (Soloway et al., 1999) and also extends to community colleges and four-year institutions. Mobile learning has been defined by the eLearning Guild as "any activity that allows individuals to be more productive when consuming, interact-ing with, or creating information, mediated through a compact digital portable device that the individual carries on a regular basis, has reliable connectivity, and fits in a pocket or purse" (Wexler et al., 2007, p. 5).

Current research documents the value of *m-learning* (learning with the assis-tance of mobile devices), which is facilitated by the technology that is already in the hands of many of our learners (Attewell, 2005; Quinn, 2012: Wagner, 2008). One of the research findings is that mobile learning "facilitates both individual and collaborative learning experiences . . . [and] can help to raise self-confidence and self-esteem by recognising uncelebrated skills, enabling non-threatening, personalised learning experiences and enabling peer-to-peer learning and support" (Attewell, 2005, p. 2). This finding supports the concept of collaborative engagement. The future of this instructional resource has yet to be determined: "m-learning may be the living laboratory for figuring out what technologies can do to engage learners, enable new capabilities, and inspire creative thinking where learning and performance support is concerned" (Wagner, 2008, p. 3). The concept of pocket-size learning environments is a reality, and the potential methods of engagement in any learning environment are limited only by the speed of the available network connection and the instructor's and students' innovative approaches.

SUMMARY

A key to effective learner engagement is for the instructor and course activities to encourage online students to take an increased responsibility for their learning. Similarly, the instructor needs to assume an increased responsibility for providing guidance and support. To engage students in a collaborative interaction, the instructor needs to model a high level of engagement through her or his exchanges within the learning environment. As instructors adapt, online students are also changing. The student population continues to represent an increased number of nontraditional adult learners who are juggling online courses with family and outside pressures. An effective online instructor determines appropriate communication strategies, manages time demands, defines her or his evolving role as an online instructor, and establishes a presence within the online classroom. Engagement strategies that consider the impact of social networking, m-learning technology, and the goal of learning as a transformational experience are critical in today's environment.

This chapter has presented an overview of the foundations of engagement that have brought us to this instructional moment in time. The importance of understanding the ever-changing world of our learning environments, the expanding opportunities, and our diverse students is critical for the success of online instruction. The concept of transformative reflection will be developed even further in Chapter 2, as it forms an essential part of the new fifth phase in the Phases of Engagement model (Conrad & Donaldson, 2004, 2011).

Evolution of the Phases of Engagement

*We want students to share our enthusiasm for our academic
discipline and find our courses so compelling that they willingly,
in fact enthusiastically, devote their hearts
and minds to the learning process.*

Barkley, 2010, p. 5

The Phases of Engagement model (Conrad & Donaldson, 2004, 2011) provides an instructional strategy for guiding students through levels of increased collaborative engagement by incorporating appropriate activities. The stages for creating an effective online learning environment span the continuum from the student as an individual to the student immersed in a collaborative learning community. The course begins with introductory one-to-one student-to-student and student-to-instructor interaction. The model uses activities to transition to a collaborative emphasis where the students actively interact to accomplish shared goals and carry this behavior into future learning experiences and career endeavors.

An important aspect of the Phases of Engagement model is that the instructor's role becomes less intrusive as the students take an increased responsibility for their learning and for meeting the course's learning objectives. The Phases of Engagement were designed to create a collaborative learning community that is adaptive to future events and perspectives. In addition, "ingenuity might be required to use the techniques in a distance setting, but the result offers opportunities to broaden and invigorate the educational experience for both student and teacher" (Herring & Smaldino, 2005, p. 4). The challenge is for the instructor to embrace and celebrate the possibilities and to communicate the meaning of the phases to learners.

In response to the experiences of the authors and the theories explained in Chapter 1, the model has continued to evolve. Current scholarly writings and research studies also verify the validity of the model (Barbour, n.d.; Parra, 2011). The updated Phases of Engagement (see Table 2.1) include the original four phases, with a new title for each one that indicates the primary purpose of each. In addition, a new fifth phase, "Continue," has been added. The purpose of this phase is to promote learner-led engagement beyond one course experience and encourage learners to incorporate it into all their learning experiences. The model, as presented in Table 2.1, continues to name the roles for the instructor and student, the process for incorporating activities, as well as suggested examples of activities for each phase. The elements from the table are explained on a phase-by-phase basis in the sections following the table, and activities to use in each phase are included in Chapters 5 through 9.

PHASE 1: CONNECT

The initial phase of the model provides a means for the student to become familiar with the instructor's expectations and the online environment. The first week or two in an online learning environment can be overwhelming for a student new to the technology and personal online interaction. It is critical that the student spend the introductory time learning to navigate through the course management system (CMS) and begin to connect with others in the course site through

Table 2.1. Phases of Engagement

Phase	Instructor Role	Student Role	Process	Activity Categories
1. Connect	Social negotiator	Newcomer (individual student)	Activities are interactive and allow learners to become acquainted. Instructor provides expectations for engagement, orientation to the course, and keeps learners on track on a one-to-one basis.	Icebreakers, individual introductions, discussion re: community issues (such as netiquette)
2. Communicate	Structural engineer	Peer partner (two-student pairing)	Instructor forms student dyads and provides activities requiring critical thinking, reflection, and sharing of ideas.	Peer reviews, activity critiques, pro-and-con discussions
3. Collaborate	Facilitator	Team member (three- to five-member groups)	Groups formed of three to five students. Groups collaborate, solve problems, and reflect on experiences; also establish a group contract on group expectations; and determine final group project.	Content discussion, role playing, debates, jigsaws
4. Co-Facilitate	Community member/subject matter expert	Initiator/partner (continued member of same group)	Activities are learner-initiated or learner-led. Learners direct discussion and facilitate interaction. Projects are developed collaboratively with instructor guidance.	Group presentations and authentic projects, learner-facilitated discussions
5. Continue	Supporter	Contemplator	Activities are focused on the transformation of the online learner that has occurred as a result of engagement activities.	Self-reflections, evaluation of course engagement, plans for future engagement

nongraded tasks. The primary activity during the first phase has the instructor requiring the students to introduce themselves and determine shared interests or experiences. This is commonly known as an *icebreaker*.

Boettcher and Conrad (2010) suggest having two types of icebreakers: social and cognitive. The social icebreaker can be more social-oriented and is conducted primarily among colleagues, while the cognitive icebreaker can be more course-oriented and occurs with the instructor. This could include requesting the completion of a skills-survey activity identifying existing student gaps in technical knowledge and online experiences. Having each student provide a digital picture or video (either of him- or herself or something meaningful in his or her life) to share with others is recommended as an initial task to help give students a sense of presence. This is also the time for the instructor to introduce her- or himself to create a sense of presence. One way this instructor presence is initiated is through the use of a welcome letter or a short introductory video. The key is to create a nurturing and safe environment for the student where her or his input is encouraged and valued.

PHASE 2: COMMUNICATE

Once the student-to-faculty and student-to-student connections are established, the focus needs to shift to creating an atmosphere that encourages a deeper level of communication between students. During the second phase, students are paired with one other student to begin exploring course content through a variety of activities. It is important that the student pairing (or dyad) be determined by the instructor, as students often do not know each other well at this early point in the course. Asking each learner to interact with someone new is a beginning step to initiating the discovery of shared interests and encouraging a diversity of perspectives within the interactions. The icebreaker from Phase 1 can provide a basis for forming the peer partners. Look for those who have already established a connection in a social icebreaker or who have expressed similar goals in a cognitive icebreaker.

Of particular importance is encouraging students to state differing views and to come to consensus on those areas of negotiated agreement. For some students, it is a revelation to learn that differences of opinion are encouraged and can be successfully expressed. Too often students working together for the first time fall prey to what may be termed the "nice" factor. In an effort not to offend a new acquaintance, students may hesitate to express true feelings or opposing ideas. The instructor needs to establish an atmosphere where lively interaction and discussion are encouraged. One way to provide an example of this approach is by having one of the dyads (perhaps one that has had previous online experience) post their spirited comments early in the discussion area. Another way is to establish a rubric for the activity. This tool is discussed further in Chapter 4.

PHASE 3: COLLABORATE

The collaborative online experience provides an opportunity for individual personal growth and learning that go beyond the experiences of the solitary learner interacting with just the content and instructor. However, collaboration has both positive and negative aspects that need to be recognized by an instructor. In an ineffective face-to-face classroom, a student can sit in class without participating for the duration of the semester and fail to have a voice in her or his learning process. This should not be possible in a collaborative online setting. There are no lurkers in a well-designed online course.

Instructors need to keep in mind that not all students embrace working within a learning community. Past negative group experiences may shadow their willingness to embrace participating in a subsequent team effort. Since "collaborative work requires bringing together information, ideas, solutions, and opinions that are not always compatible with one another" (Schellens & Valcke, 2006, p. 350), crafting effective teams is critical. The Phases of Engagement model fosters individual knowledge acquisition by creating effective online collaborative teams.

Phase 3 of the model begins with the instructor assigning team members for the remaining part of the course by combining the dyads from Phase 2. Groups should not select their own members, because they tend not to be as diverse or scholarly with self-selection. The formation of the group is a craft unto itself. The instructor uses the characteristics of the individual class members that are identified during the first phase with the icebreakers and continues with the dyad assignment. Project or small-group discussion teams should consist of three to five members, including only one with leadership responsibilities (which can be rotated) and at least one member with strong technical skills. A group consisting of five leaders normally will be bogged down in power struggles; a group of five followers will be waiting for external guidance to move forward, and a group with no technical skills will flounder. The artistry comes in the instructor finding the right balance between each of the leadership characteristics and learner skills.

As soon as teams are formed, a team-building activity is advised. This can be a short icebreaker that can be more academic in nature and is just for the team. The creation of an agreed-upon group contract is the next task after the team-building activity. If posting times are not stated or alternatives are not determined for missed deadlines due to personal challenges, the group will experience a high level of stress. The early posters tend to lose patience with the consistently late posters to discussions and tasks. Determining the group's expectations early in the third phase will help alleviate some of this frustration. In the case where the instructor sets the activity expectations, learners still should be given the opportunity to modify them, if at all possible.

The types of assignments normally included in this phase are group projects and discussions. Rubrics for grading these tasks need to be shared early in the course and used for grading throughout the course. Since there is a tendency for some students to rely upon others to do the majority of the work in a group project, it is important that rubrics include documentation of an individual's contribution. A peer evaluation process at the end of the course also helps in evaluating a student's work and attitude from the perspective the team. This is discussed further in Chapter 4.

When working with the collaborative groups, it is important to remember to encourage final projects that represent authentic tasks that can be implemented after the course ends. Students are intrinsically motivated and find value in a project that can live beyond the time in the class. An authentic project should include tasks in the required final documentation that can be incorporated into a learner's current or future employment or community involvement.

PHASE 4: CO-FACILITATE

This phase of the model is centered on moving students to the role of co-facilitating their own learning experience. The collaborative group is expected to lead content-related discussions and to facilitate team member interactions. Most of this phase of a course is focused on a final project that was determined collaboratively in Phase 3 by the learners. The instructor steps down to assume the role of a fellow team member at this point in the class and to offer guidance, when needed, from the perspective of a subject matter expert (SME).

A successful collaborative effort that has implemented a Phase 4 level of engagement is one that has a lasting effect on the learner and instructor. The saying that "the whole is greater than the parts" has never been truer than when a successful collaborative effort has met the team's shared learning goals and vision. This level of interactivity and personal responsibility for learning has the ability to empower students and enforce the importance of being a lifelong learner.

PHASE 5: CONTINUE

The ultimate goal of using the Phases of Engagement model is to empower learners to increase their engagement as instructor guidance diminishes. Once a learner has co-facilitated in a learning environment, the opportunity can provide a starting point for her or his next learning experience. For example, some students who have taken several courses with us have become leaders of the icebreaking activity in subsequent courses with us. However, learners need to realize that they are ready for such an undertaking and need to develop a way to demonstrate more leadership and engagement from the very beginning of the next learning opportunity.

Activities in Phase 5 need to help students realize that they have been "transformed" and are indeed more engaged with the learning process, more of a leader than when they entered the course, and that they have the power to be leaders in future learning experiences. The type of activity most useful in this phase is reflective in nature and can be done as a final course activity with feedback provided by the instructor as a form of course wrap-up.

APPROPRIATE ACTIVITIES

The choice of appropriate activities is important for the successful transition of students through each phase of the model. It is important to identify activities that include a sharing of personal experiences, reflection of student learning and opinions, and interaction focused on issues related to course content and understanding. Keep in mind that activities for the sake of fun only create disgruntled students when they occur beyond the first phase. The instructor's awareness of the students' level of engagement within the model will assist in determining which activities are appropriate. Many face-to-face activities can be successfully converted to the online delivery mode. The instructor must determine which activities will match the specified learning objectives while challenging each student to think in new ways and from diverse perspectives.

Many individuals may be initially overwhelmed by the technical skills and by the amount of time necessary for success in the online classroom. One way to overcome this difficulty is by matching the appropriate activity to the learners' levels of skill and willingness to interact. A benefit of the activity-driven approach is the realization of self-efficacy (one's own belief in her or his ability to do well). By taking small steps, each with an increasing number of supportive individual interactions, students begin to engage in the spirit of collaboration. Appropriate phase-determined activities also encourage a level of reflection on the learning process and individual growth. "Providing time for students to think, talk, and write about their learning, their current level of skill development, their effective use of strategies, and their goal achievement is essential for developing self-efficacy" (Eisenberger, Conti-D'Antonio, & Bertrando, 2005, p. 52).

There are many social networking tools available to assist the group's interaction in Phases 3 and 4: "social tools are emerging which permit rapid exchange of knowledge, and high levels of dialogue. Communication can now occur collaboratively (wiki or online meetings), through individual broadcast (blogs, podcasts, or video logs), and in shared spaces (social bookmarking)" (Siemens, 2006, p. 15). Shared documentation on Google Docs and group chats through Skype voice interaction are other examples of tools that enhance collaboration and co-facilitation activities.

The team's final collaborative effort in meeting the course's learning objectives is demonstrated through a group presentation with supporting documentation. Creativity in group presentations is encouraged in an online setting. Some of the group presentations could include an interactive experience in Second Life (a virtual world), an energetic YouTube video, and an Adobe Connect shared presentation with PowerPoint. Regardless of the delivery choice, ensure that all class members have access to the software and hardware for the chosen delivery method selected.

Adding the concept of engagement to an online course can make the move to online seem daunting. However, simply begin by using engagement one phase at a time. Just incorporate an icebreaker in your course and form study groups for the first offering of your online course. The next offering can include a dyad activity or group discussion, with the offering after that providing an additional team project. Building slowly will provide an opportunity for you to observe how learners are reacting in a particular phase and how you might improve the activity before moving on to incorporating the next phase's activities.

Designing an online course is an evolving process, so don't feel as if everything has to be perfect the first time around. Ask learners for their opinions about the interaction in the course, and you may be surprised to find they are appreciative of what you have done initially and will provide suggestions for further improvements. Involve them in the design of the course—that's engagement as well as empowerment!

SUMMARY

The purpose of the Phases of Engagement is to provide a method to ease learners into learning how to collaborate and take responsibility for their own knowledge generation. The model defines the roles of the instructor and students in each phase and describes the type of activities to consider incorporating in each particular phase. Be sure to align activities with learning objectives, learner readiness, and learning needs.

While phases can be added incrementally to a course with each additional offering, skipping phases is not recommended. Even when the learners have been together as a cohort in a previous course, the instructor may be unfamiliar to the students. There may be individual students who are becoming more comfortable in an online environment and need to explore the interpersonal relationships with others as it progresses through each of the activity-driven phases. While deleting a phase is not recommended, moving quickly through a phase may work well. Or, in the case of cohorts, asking learners to lead earlier in the course may also prove effective.

The key throughout the Phases of Engagement is to remember that it is about the students' learning. The richness that is possible through collaborative engagement often surpasses what is seen in a traditional face-to-face classroom. Do not hesitate to take a risk and seek the deeper levels of engagement. Continually reinforce the idea to students of being proactive participants in their own learning progression.

The next chapter focuses on the various aspects to consider when implementing the Phases of Engagement, including how to provide timely communication and manage engagement in large classes.

Implementing the Phases of Engagement

An excellent online instructor will know how to get the process started, facilitate it effectively, and then get out of the way and observe the results, jumping in as a resource to share expertise when necessary and to guide the process.

Palloff & Pratt, 2011, p. 10

While the Phases of Engagement model offers a step-by-step approach to increasing learner involvement, it still requires planning in order to weave it appropriately into a course. Will you begin to incorporate engagement in a fully online environment or one that is blended? Will you use some of the phases or all of the phases at once? How you will manage engagement in a large class? What will you do if something is not working as planned? What will you do if learners are resistant to engagement? How will you handle difficult students? How will you avoid being consumed by interaction? These are the questions addressed in this chapter.

ONLINE OR BLENDED?

Instructors and instructional designers deal with many choices when selecting the methodology for online delivery. The traditional all-or-nothing approach has morphed into an increased occurrence of a blended approach. A blended delivery option allows a portion of the class sessions to continue face-to-face (f2f) while some tasks are completed through online interactions and postings. For the novice online student or instructor, a blended environment is a recommended approach that combines the benefits of each of the instructional strategies.

One approach for implementing a modified blended approach for online course implementation is as follows:

- First meeting of class as f2f. The instructor defines expectations, provides a course overview, describes assignments with associated rubrics, and provides an orientation to the online course management tool and tips on how to learn online. Students introduce themselves using an online icebreaker activity.

- Final meeting of class as f2f. The final class is an opportunity for collaborative groups to present their final projects and celebrate the course. Food and a final summative activity should be a part of the celebration as well as administration of the course evaluation.

- In between the first and last f2f meetings. Conduct a weekly synchronous chat during the weeks that are not f2f or an asynchronous discussion. Class members could meet f2f for team meetings or activities such as a class debate presenting diverse perspectives on the course content to date. This might also be an opportunity to invite a guest speaker to share their experiences related to the course content.

When modifying f2f activities and assignments for the online learning environment, it is important to identify activities that include a sharing of personal experiences, reflection of student learning and opinions, and interaction focused on issues related to course content and understanding. Not every classroom activity can be transformed to online, and instructors may want to refer to the suggested activities in Chapters 5 through 9 of this book for additional ideas.

Activities for the online portion of the class will change as learners progress through the Phases of Engagement model. The interactions of most online course communications are the discussion postings (examples include threaded discussions, blog postings, Skype, and chat forums). Require students to review course content through assigned readings, video presentations, or audio tracks. Direct the discussion using carefully crafted questions, leading the learner to delve deeper into the subject matter. One recommended approach is to have the students post individual responses during the first week and then respond to others in their collaborative group during the second week. The final step of this process is to have the group come to consensus on the discussion questions and then have the assigned facilitator for the team post the final agreed-upon responses. Each member of the team should be assigned the role of group facilitator by the instructor at least once during Phases 3 and 4.

Whether you choose to ease into the online learning environment gradually or jump in all at once, planning and effective communication are key. Table 3.1 is one example of a course planning tool that can be used to envision both instructional and engagement activities.

ENGAGING LARGE CLASSES

The thought of motivating a large class to interact, and then managing that high level of engagement, can seem daunting to even the most experienced online instructor. However, if one thinks of a large online course as a class with numerous sections, you can begin to see that a large engaged class is indeed possible.

Consider breaking the class into sections by last name for the icebreaker in Phase 1 with the Phase 2 dyads spinning off from each icebreaker group. Further small-group and team formation needed for Phase 3 and beyond can be determined as they would be with smaller class sizes, based on common interests, experiences, work patterns, and/or location. In a large class, there will be so many teams that an instructor may feel that she or he will never know what each one is doing. That is where team contracts, team reporting, and team member evaluations are particularly important.

Table 3.1. Engaged Course Planning Tool

Cognitive or Engagement Objective	Phase of Engagement	Content (Readings, Video, Audio)	Activity Directions	Communication of Directions (Syllabus, Assignments Area, Discussion, Wiki, Blog Areas)	Rubric Components

A team contract can be developed by the team itself or a template can be provided by the instructor. If a team contract is not used, then a team member evaluation or rubric outlining the essential characteristics of a good team member should be provided by the instructor. With a large class, consider requiring several team reports during the course so that you can see how the team is developing. Step in only if asked and only once the team has tried to resolve problems themselves. Encourage and motivate as needed, but be careful not to dominate the team activity.

MANAGING ENGAGEMENT

Using the Phases of Engagement helps manage the course by indicating what interaction level should be introduced at a given point in a course. Learners are not expected to immediately be at a high level of engagement, so an instructor does not have to struggle with full engagement right at the beginning of a course. This helps in managing a course.

In addition, today's course management systems (CMS) such as Blackboard and Moodle provide *at-a-glance* tools to see when learners are participating within a course. Use these tools to monitor and then remind learners that they need to participate in the course.

The one area that still requires a great deal of instructor time and management is developing the qualitative aspect of engagement. Key aspects indicating the level of quality in engagement that need to be considered are: Did learners apply key knowledge? Did they expand the discussion with new ideas or solutions? Did they critically analyze one another's contributions? Did they provide additional scholarly references to support statements of research results or expert opinions? One way to manage the review of discussion posts is to quickly scan initial posts to see if there is a basic reply to the question. Then either respond to those needing the most quality improvement or, if this is more than 40 percent of the class, post a response to the entire class with additional questions that deepen their discussion. Also, rotate who you respond to in discussions each week and, if you find yourself needing to respond to the same students who are missing the point, schedule a phone conference to discuss how they need to improve their discussion participation.

Managing engagement can be easier using the Phases of Engagement and CMS tools because these tools enable the bulk of time to be devoted to determining what level of quality has been reached in the interaction. The tasks that an instructor needs to consider include:

- Determine the engagement activities for each cognitive or engagement objective
- Design the grading rubric for each activity as needed
- Incorporate multiple perspective assessment for team activities through a team contract and/or peer evaluation
- Explain the guidelines for interaction to learners in the syllabus and provide an audio introduction to the course
- Set up the activities and provide multiple descriptions of the activities, including grading, in the syllabus and the course area in which the activity will take place
- Provide frequent feedback to learners regarding their engagement level and the quality of their contributions to the knowledge development process
- Ask learners periodically for their feedback on their individual engagement and the engagement of their colleagues in course activities
- Note revisions needed to activities, directions, and participation guidelines as they occur so that you are ready to revise the course for the next offering

TIMELY COMMUNICATION

Timely communication from the educator to the student is a critical component of instructor engagement. Finkelstein (2006) emphasizes the research findings that prompt feedback is of critical importance in an online setting that lacks traditional verbal cues. Use these guidelines for ensuring timely feedback:

- All technical questions are responded to within twenty-four hours, even if only letting the student know the inquiry was forwarded to the proper person for resolution
- All student course questions are answered within forty-eight hours
- All written course assignments are graded and returned within seven calendar days

- Major written assignments, such as major papers or projects, need to be returned within fourteen calendar days

The same expectations for task completion that are placed upon students need to be placed upon the instructor. Students should be given clear guidelines regarding task deadlines. The instructor needs to model adherence to a set time frame and provide constructive feedback. Cavanaugh's (2009) research indicates that a successful online experience depends on the quality of interactions between instructors and students.

Devise an audio or e-mail feedback template such as the one in Table 3.2 or based on the activity rubric so that you are simply adding comments instead of writing feedback anew for each learner.

Table 3.2. Feedback Template

Salutation	Dear [Student Name], I've reviewed your submittal of Assignment 1 and have a few comments for you.
What worked well?	Your introduction to the project was excellent, as was the outline of the major aspects to be covered in the presentation.
What needs additional work based on the rubric, assessment plan, or learning objective?	The project could have been improved in the following ways: Or Elements that detracted from the project are as follows:
Closing	Your final grade for this assignment is [grade]. If you have any questions about my comments, I will be in my online office tomorrow evening. If that is not convenient, please contact me to schedule an appointment. Best regards, [Instructor Name]

INSTRUCTOR TIME MANAGEMENT

Time management is a monumental consideration when teaching online. The challenge is to find the balance between fulfilling professional needs and responding effectively to student demands. Early burnout is a potential result when boundaries are not set to ensure instructor survival and reduce stress. In their 2011 book *Managing Online Instructor Workload*, Conceicao and Lehman provide a template for managing tasks and prioritizing time that can also be used when incorporating the Phases of Engagement (see Table 3.3).

In addition, here are several suggested strategies for reducing the requirement for instructor time based on the work of Conceicao and Lehman (2011) and Boettcher and Conrad (2010):

- Time limit: Determine how much time you will spend "in class" per day—for example, one hour in the morning and one hour at night. If you are grading assignments, remind your students of this and state that you will be checking messages but won't be in the discussion until grading has been completed.

- Broadcast: share responses that may affect more than one student to reduce repeated questions.

- Anticipate: use the FAQ (frequently asked questions) approach by posting responses to common questions

Table 3.3. Template for Managing Tasks and Prioritizing Time

Course Sequence	Type of Task	Week Number	Estimated Time Spent
Before	Design		
During and at the end of the course	Administrative		
	Facilitative		
	Evaluative		

Source: From *Managing Online Instructor Workload: Strategies for Finding Balance and Success,* by S.C.O. Conceicao and R. M. Lehman, 2011, Jossey-Bass.

- Facilitate: assign a rotating student facilitator to report the results of a group consensus. This results in the instructor creating only a single group response.

- Inform: post information on instructor availability in advance.

- Delegate: assign tech buddies between students to allow the computer technology hurdles to be resolved without instructor involvement

- Redirect: don't hesitate to direct students to additional resources in order to prompt students to engage in levels of higher thinking

- Breathe: take two days off at the midpoint of a course for some personal time or identify one day a week that you will not be in the class. Let students know of your unavailability.

CHANGING COURSE

Every course should maintain some level of flexibility in assignments and activities without compromising the learning objectives. An activity should not only engage learners but should be as authentic and relevant to a learner as possible. A door should be left open in the event a learner or cohort of learners comes along who find a particular activity or set of activities meaningless. In the event that learners express a desire to do a different activity, listen with an open mind and revise the activity, if possible.

Changing an activity requires that the instructor and learners come to consensus quickly. The instructor needs to communicate the recommended change and require a quick response from learners or move on with the activity as planned. If a majority of learners respond timely in support of the change, move ahead with it. This can result in a far more motivated learning community and an activity that was far better than the one originally planned.

In some cases, transitioning learners from one phase of engagement to the next may require additional attention. Sometimes learners become stuck on a particular activity such as an icebreaker. You may need to remind them that the activity has ended or you may wish to continue the activity in another way. For example, tie the icebreaker to the team formation and ask learners why they think they make a good team, judging by the icebreaker information. Another way to move learners to the next discussion is to post a message thanking them for their participation in the summary of the discussion and urging them on to the next module or activity.

ONLINE EDUCATOR'S "BILL OF RIGHTS"

It's good to remember that even though we strive for a student-centered learning environment, an online educator has a right to a life as well. Engaging your students can become life-consuming if their lives are allowed to take precedence over your own. By this we mean that students often have reasons, many of them valid, why they are unable to meet a particular interaction guideline. While an instructor can be sympathetic to a learner, it is a good idea to set guidelines for expectations and stick to them. If timeliness is an issue periodically due to illness or professional demands, it should not critically harm the learner's grade. However, if a learner is consistently late posting comments or participating in team activities, there should be established consequences.

To promote team independence and diminish the necessity for instructor intervention, ask learners to consult one another before asking you for the answer. This can be done in your online office area. Learners can post questions in that area, but you can instruct everyone that it is an open area for anyone to answer. You can then confirm or expand on answers provided by the learning community. This is a great approach for questions such as "When is that due?"

Remember to post the times you are available and require that students respect your time boundaries. In today's world, sometimes a learner can tell that you are online and may feel free to *chat* with you, even though it is outside your office hours and you are in the midst of grading. Remind students that unless it is an emergency (as in their assignment is due in a few hours), they should contact you during office hours or should set up an appointment to talk first thing the next day.

Above all, treat learners with professional courtesy and require the same from them. If you have asked them a question in the discussion, remind them that you would like a response. If their life circumstances are particularly difficult and prevent them from fulfilling the requirements for the course, counsel them on how they can improve their performance and what options might be available to them, but don't allow their problems to become yours. Also, request that you are notified of a potential problem before it begins affecting the student's performance. Learning from a *silent* student of a sick child or crashed hard drive three days after an assignment due date is frustrating for the instructor who is striving to complete timely grading.

DEALING WITH DIFFICULT STUDENTS

For some reason, an attitude of bullying and rudeness has been growing online. This may be due to the brevity of some communication forms, such as Twitter, or it may be due to the fact that we cannot see one another's reactions and do not realize the damage our terse comments elicit. Also, limiting communication to textual interactions prevents the nonverbal communication elements that are so informative in our daily conversations.

When a learner is rude in a learning community or to you as the instructor, it's a good idea to first assume that they did not mean it as it is being taken. The next step is to then schedule an audio conference either via phone or Skype to talk with the student. Don't exchange anything text-based with the learner about this matter, because the misunderstandings may just continue and even escalate. When talking with the learner, discuss how the tone of their comments might be taken when read by others and how that tone can be improved. They might want to read their comments out loud or simply explain the emotions behind them by writing things such as "this may sound as if I'm angry, but I'm not—just curious." Defuse these types of situations quickly, as they can weaken or destroy overall levels of engagement.

SUMMARY

Using the Phases of Engagement model is one way to minimize the stress of incorporating and managing online interaction. By introducing engagement to the learners with a Phase 1 icebreaker and then moving learners toward working together in the remaining phases, an instructor provides opportunities for learners to learn to engage and become more self-directed in that engagement. This approach results in reducing the time usually spent cajoling learners to interact. Other tools that diminish the time spent managing engagement are learner contracts, rubrics, and team member evaluations. Providing clear guidelines regarding engagement expectations helps learners to perform at a maximum level.

In addition to learner guidelines, the instructor is also entitled to set boundaries for his or her engagement with learners. Setting office hours and sticking to them so that learners cannot simply engage with you at all hours, whenever they discover you online, provides the space you need to grade and develop new aspects of the course. Online learning should not consume the lives of learners *or* instructors!

Chapter 4 discusses the assessment of online engagement. Considerations to be discussed include whether to use a written or performance-based assessment and how to assess in phases.

Assessing Online Engaged Learning

If the assessments are opportunities for students to learn, then we [instructors] are using every opportunity to refine their knowledge as well as evaluate and refine our course.

Smith, 2008, p. 34

Assessment in any type of course, online or classroom-based, is either written or performance-based. Written assessment is best to use when evaluating declarative knowledge (that which can be stated) and procedural knowledge (knowing how to do something). Problem-solving ability is best assessed with performance-based methods. Learners can work together to process and develop any of these types of knowledge.

When considering an online engaged environment, typically in Phases 1 and 2, learners are getting to know one another and most likely developing declarative and procedural knowledge. In this case, a written assessment to determine whether the learning objectives have been met would be appropriate.

In Phases 3 and 4, learners are most likely involved in achieving learning objectives that involve problem solving. With this type of knowledge acquisition, there is no one path to the solution, but the process requires critical thinking and the application of rules and knowledge developed in the prior phases. In this stage, performance assessments are most appropriate to determine whether the learning objectives have been met.

Phase 5 focuses on how learners will carry the concept of engagement forward in their future learning experiences. While not explicitly associated with learning objectives, using performance assessment to ensure the reflection process is diligently undertaken is a good idea.

There is also the concern about the engagement process itself. Is it working? Are learners involved? Answering these key questions requires some type of performance assessment as well.

DEVELOPING A WRITTEN ASSESSMENT FOR ONLINE ENGAGED LEARNING

Written assessments for engaged learning activities that are developing declarative and procedural knowledge can be done in the traditional manner via tests. They should be based on the learning objectives and developed using an assessment plan that states the written assessment item associated with each objective (see Table 4.1).

Table 4.1. Example of Assessment Plan Format

Performance Objective	Assessment Type (True or False, Multiple Choice, or Other)	Assessment Item	Additional Comments

One cannot think of using online written assessments without considering the possibility of cheating and academic dishonesty. This can be minimized with strategies such as rotating questions from a database, limiting the time for the test, and password-only access. However, it can also be limited by making sure that written assessments are not the only type of assessment used.

In an online engaged learning environment, the process of engagement itself plays a role in how well information is processed and knowledge is developed. Therefore, it too must be part of the assessment. However, because engagement is a process that has no one path, a performance assessment as discussed in the next section should be developed in addition to the written assessment.

DEVELOPING A PERFORMANCE ASSESSMENT FOR ONLINE ENGAGED LEARNING

When problem solving is being evaluated, a performance assessment should be used. This type of assessment looks at either a process or a product as demonstrating the problem-solving ability of the individual. If a group product is produced, it is important to consider what role engagement and collaboration, or lack thereof, played in the quality of the product.

Assessing online engagement can be tricky. Because we cannot see all that goes into learners interacting with one another, it can sometimes be difficult to quantify what has occurred. Who has led and who has opted out? Who really knows the content, and who is just benefiting from the knowledge of others? How well has the team functioned and assisted in the learning process? This is where the need for multiple-perspective assessment comes into play (Oosterhof, Conrad, & Ely, 2008).

Multiple-perspective assessment recognizes that no one point of view can tell the entire story of engagement and assess it appropriately. Rather, the views of the instructor, the team, the individual, and in some cases the learning community are all needed to paint the picture of engaged learning. Figure 4.1 illustrates how these four perspectives fit together to provide an effective means of assessing engaged learning.

The instructor usually observes the knowledge understanding and application demonstrated, but the team can shed light on whether the entire team is

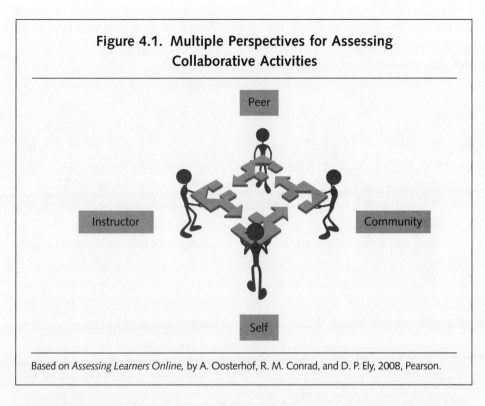

Figure 4.1. Multiple Perspectives for Assessing Collaborative Activities

Peer

Instructor

Community

Self

Based on *Assessing Learners Online,* by A. Oosterhof, R. M. Conrad, and D. P. Ely, 2008, Pearson.

demonstrating the knowledge or just a few. Finally, the individual also provides information on what she or he is able to demonstrate as a result of the engaged collaborative learning.

In addition to viewing the engagement through the eyes of all those involved, it is also important to utilize the basic principles of assessment by asking:

• Did the engaged activity fulfill the objective?

• Are both the process and product being assessed?

• Did the rubric describe all the behaviors and requirements of the assignment?

The timing of assessment is also important. Assessment can be done on a formative basis while instruction is occurring or on a summative basis at the end of the course. With engaged activities, it is important to examine not only the product development but the process as well. Both the product and process should be assessed formatively and summatively. Product assessment can be accomplished with a rubric that describes the desired product and then describes less desirable versions of the product that are worth fewer points.

GRADING

A performance assessment of engagement can be graded using a rubric that lists each objective or criterion and describes the performance level required. Characteristics to consider including in an engaged activity rubric are depth of thought, timeliness of response, recognition of others' thoughts, and adding new knowledge to the conversation. In other words, learners must realize they are building a conversation and must exhibit thinking beyond simply agreeing with the other discussion posts by contributing thoughts that help develop the content in new ways for others and that are respectful of others' time by posting in the time frame requested. A rubric takes time to develop, but in the long run can provide quicker feedback. It can also serve as a checklist for learners in assessing their own product or engagement level and to make adjustments to better meet the grading criteria before a final grade is assigned. Table 4.2 is one example of such a rubric.

Developing and using group rubrics that recognize individual contributions is an effective way to assess a learner's contribution. Some instructors choose to weight an individual's contribution on a group project by assigning it 25 to 50 percent of the final individual grade. This approach may prevent one or two students from doing the majority of the work while all group members receive the identical final project grade. Items for assessing the individual's contribution may include written documentation on the learner's project responsibilities, reflection on the learning experience, suggestions for implementation of the project into her or his current or future work environment, or discussions on team interactions that inform the individual on her or his learning style. A final consideration for determining the final rubric-based score for an individual's contribution is the use of an anonymous peer evaluation. Items that are commonly assessed on a peer evaluation form are timeliness of contributions (including attending team meetings), quality of contribution, and quality of collaboration with others (such as being open to others' ideas and attending team meetings). Exhibit 4.1 is one example of a peer evaluation form.

Table 4.2. Issues Paper Rubric: Grading (250 Possible Points)

Criterion	Description	25	20	15	10	Points
Paper is organized and well prepared Possible points: 0–50	Organization	Paper logically organized and well prepared with documented support for the conclusions presented.	Paper logically organized, but conclusions weakly supported by Literature Review section.	Paper logically organized, but conclusions not supported by Literature Review section.	Paper not organized and no documented support for the Conclusion.	25
	Structure	Structure includes: Introduction, Literature Review, Conclusions and Recommendations, and References. Guidelines are followed.	Structure includes: Introduction, Literature Review, Conclusions and Recommendations, and References. Only two of the sections follow the guidelines.	Structure includes: Introduction, Literature Review, Conclusions and Recommendations, and References. Only one of the sections follows the guidelines.	Structure does not include all of the following: Introduction, Literature Review, Conclusions and Recommendations, and References. Sections do not follow the guidelines.	25

Continued

Table 4.2. *Continued*

Criterion	Description	25	20	15	10	Points
Key concepts adequately presented Possible points: 0–50	Concepts	Key concepts presented with supporting outside resources. The paper demonstrates knowledge beyond the chapter readings and discussions.	Key concepts presented with supporting outside resources.	Failed to present all of the related concepts. Outdated outside resources were used.	Failed to present concepts or misrepresented several major concepts.	50
Conclusions and Recommendations Possible points: 0–50	Summarization and Future Research	The literature reviewed is summarized and related back to the original issue. The impact of this issue on real-world situations is presented with supporting references and examples. Future areas for further research are also included.	The literature reviewed is summarized and related back to the original issue. The impact of this topic on real-world situations is presented with supporting references and examples. Future areas for further research are also included.	The literature reviewed is summarized. The impact of this topic on real-world situations is presented without supporting references and examples. Future areas for further research are not included.	The literature reviewed is summarized, but does not relate back to the original issue. The impact of this topic on real-world situations is missing. Future areas for further research are not included.	50

Criterion	Description	25	20	15	10	Points
Adequate number of references Possible points: 0–50	References	Over ten appropriate references have been cited.	A minimum of ten references have been cited appropriately within the paper.	Less than seven appropriate references have been cited.	No valid references have been cited.	25
	APA Formatting and Citation	Paper is written in APA format. Correct formatting of headings, citations, references, quotes, fonts, type sizes, and so on.	Paper is close to being written in APA format. Correct formatting is evident in four of the following: headings, citations, references, quotes, fonts, and type sizes.	Paper is close to being written in APA format. Correct formatting is evident in two of the following: headings, citations, references, quotes, fonts, and type sizes.	Paper is not written in APA format. Correct formatting is evident in none of the following: headings, citations, references, quotes, fonts, and type sizes.	25

Continued

Table 4.2. Continued

Criterion	Description	25	20	15	10	Points
Correct spelling and grammar Possible points: 0–25	Spelling and Grammar	Grammar, spelling, and composition of paper demonstrate graduate-level work. Evidence that spell-checker was used.	Grammar, spelling, and composition of paper below graduate-level work. Evidence that spell-checker was used.	Grammar, spelling, and composition of paper require serious additional effort to reach graduate-level work. Consider the UNI Writing Center. Evidence that spell-checker was used.	No indication that spell-checker was used. Writing level unacceptable. Student required to document a visit to UNI Writing Center for assistance.	25
Overall quality Possible points: 0–25	Quality of Insight	The paper demonstrates an understanding of the concepts beyond the printed materials. These insights are effectively stated in the paper.	The paper demonstrates an understanding of the concepts beyond the printed materials.	The paper demonstrates a limited understanding of the concepts beyond the printed materials.	The paper demonstrates no understanding of the concepts beyond the printed materials.	25
Total Score						250

Exhibit 4.1. Peer Evaluation Form

Your name _____

Name of individual being evaluated _____

Date _____

Criterion	Description	Points (10 max)
Timeliness	Completed all assignments in a timely manner. Attended team meetings unless excused.	
Collaboration	Demonstrated openness to others' ideas and willingness to include all others in project development.	
Communication	Demonstrated sensitivity in communicating with others and did so in a timely and positive manner.	
Quality	Completed all assignments to the level of quality expected by the group.	
Self-direction	Completed assigned tasks in a quality manner without unnecessary assistance by others.	
	Total (50 points max)	

Percent (%) Contribution

Estimate the percent contribution of the team member you are evaluating under the column marked "Percent Contribution by Individual" for each assignment. The percent contribution of the individual plus the percent contribution of all others *must* add up to 100 percent for each major task.

Task	Percent Contribution by Individual	Percent Contribution by All Others
Idea development		
Team meetings		
Activity or project presentation		

Additional Comments

It is important to inform the learner of the criteria for grading early in the process. When students are able to complete assignments with the rubric in front of them, surprises and frustrations are reduced once the final grade is posted. To avoid a disagreement on the final score, each student can grade her or his assignment her- or himself using the rubric and turn that in with their final assignment. This encourages each learner to use the rubric as a checklist for her or his work, as opposed to merely relying on the instructor to review the work and grade it.

PROVIDING FEEDBACK

Prompt feedback concerning the quality of an interaction is essential to learners engaging and eventually leading in the online learning environment. Feedback should be based on the posted rubric or scoring plan and provide positive suggestions for improvement. One way to provide swift feedback is to use a standard message that can be posted in the discussion or sent via e-mail based on the rubric and then tailored with specific comments to each individual or group. Feedback concerning the quality of the engagement process itself is particularly important right from the beginning of the course. Providing feedback after the first week reminds learners of the importance of interaction in the course and that interactions will be monitored.

TECHNOLOGY TO USE FOR ASSESSMENT

Most of the course management systems include assessment tools geared toward written assessments. When a performance assessment is used, using the Comment feature in Word is often adequate and has widespread use. Using audio or video to evaluate performance and/or to provide feedback is now coming into wider use. The beauty of audio or video for feedback is that it personalizes and humanizes the critique. Its use should be considered particularly in cases where significant improvement is needed in the performance and the feedback might be more negative than under normal circumstances.

Most new computers now have webcams so video feedback can be quickly recorded and sent to learners. Audio feedback can be easily accomplished through a tool such as Audacity. PowerPoint or VoiceThread can also be used to provide a one-slide summary of your feedback accompanied with audio. Products such as Jing can link an audio comment to a particular portion of a paper. This is more time-intensive than simply an audio file, but could be useful in cases where the performance was particularly poor. A test feedback message should be sent to all learners before utilizing this type of feedback to make sure that everyone's system can accommodate the audio or video file you will send. Some versions of Skype also allow for document sharing of the participant's computer desktop to allow for shared visuals of the artifact being discussed.

PHASE-BASED ASSESSMENT

In each phase of engagement, the learner has a different focus on the engagement process. Therefore, it makes sense that the assessment changes in each phase as well. Using "rolling rubrics" that change as the expectations and phases of engagement change also sends the message to learners that their engagement needs to deepen as time advances. For example, in Phase 1, learners should be assessed as newcomers to online interaction. Therefore, the focus should be on participation, and the rubric should be weighted in this direction. In Phase 2, peer partnership is the focus, so a learner *must* show up or they will fail to receive points for the activity. What is most important in this phase is that learners support each other through timely and quality posts and that they reply to one another and effectively communicate. Table 4.3 illustrates a proposed weighting of activities on a phase-by-phase basis.

USING ASSESSMENT TO IMPROVE ENGAGEMENT

It's important to examine assessment results to determine where the engagement process can be improved. Did learners follow the directions for the activity? Did learners participate or opt out of interacting with one another? Were learners confused about how to engage or the expectations? Were they timely with their interactions? Was periodic feedback provided to inform the learners of the quality of their engagement? Were the learning objectives for the activity met?

If a learning objective was not met, reexamine how well the activity matched the objectives. If the objective states that learners will demonstrate how to solve a particular problem or set of problems, did the activity or project state that? Did the rubric describe what elements would indicate whether the problem had been

Table 4.3. Assessment Focus by Phase
(with Each Activity Worth Ten Points)

Activity Type	Phase 1	Phase 2	Phase 3	Phase 4	Phase 5
Icebreaker Attributes					
Posted	4				
Timeliness	3				
Answers questions posed	3				
Peer Partner Attributes					
Posted		3			
Timeliness		3			
Contributes to furthering the discussion		4			
Group Discussion Attributes					
Participation			2	0	
Timeliness			2	3	
Processes content being covered			3	3	
Replies or furthers the discussion			3	4	
Team Project or Activity					
Timeliness				3	
Furthers the group effort				4	
Individual contribution to the group				3	
Design of Team-Led Activity					
Met objectives				6	
Went beyond objectives				2	
Used engaging techniques to involve colleagues				2	
Participation in "Continuing" Activities					
Discusses how individual knowledge increased					5
Proposes how concepts can be authentically applied					5

solved? Were the instructions for the activity clear? Was the activity relevant to the learners and the learning objectives? Did the activity build upon prior learner knowledge or experiences?

If the engagement process itself did not work, were the expectations stated clearly and in multiple places (such as the syllabus, the activity directions, and the discussion area)? Was there a rubric for participation in addition to the rubric for knowledge development? Did it describe the criteria for ideal engagement? Was feedback provided regularly that gave the learner an indication of how well they were fulfilling the rubric's criteria?

Finally, if learners did not participate in the activity, was there enough incentive to engage? Namely, were there enough points allocated to it? Whether we like it or not, some learners figure out just how much they need to complete in a course to earn an A. One way to camouflage a low number of points allocated is to take the course points for engagement and multiply them by 10 or even 100. Seeing "worth 100 points" versus "worth 10 points" psychologically establishes that engagement is of higher value.

SUMMARY

Assessment in an online engaged learning environment requires two types of assessment: one for the learning objectives and one for the learner's engagement. Using multiple-perspective assessment where the team, the individual learner, and the instructor all provide input on the quality of the engaged learning from their own viewpoints increases the likelihood that the assessment will be more valid than an approach that includes only the instructor's view. Using standard assessment tools such as an assessment plan and a rubric or scoring plan ensures that the assessment will be based on the learning objectives and that feedback will be provided promptly to maximize the engaged learning experience. The use of clearly defined tools and evaluation criteria also adds a more objective perspective to the assessment process.

This chapter concludes Part One and the discussion of the foundational elements associated with the Phases of Engagement model. In Part Two, the characteristics and examples of activities to use in each phase are presented.

Activities to Engage
Online Learners

As we did with our first book, *Engaging the Online Learner*, we asked colleagues to share their most successful online activities that engaged learners. The large number of responses we received from our colleagues across the nation was humbling. In this section we have organized the activities submitted to us according to the Phase of Engagement in which they fit best. Each chapter contains activities along with a checklist of elements to consider when designing an activity for a particular phase. We have also included a few activities that we have used ourselves. Each activity contains instructions to be posted in your online course. Use the activities as they appear in the book or modify them to best fit your course and/or content.

Phase 1 Activities: Connect

The purpose of the activities in this initial phase is to help students become comfortable with communicating online not only with the instructor but with one another as well. The primary activities in this phase are as follows:

- The social icebreaker that is a simple expression of self and focuses on the interaction among learners

- The cognitive icebreaker that focuses on academic and professional goals as well as the interaction between the learners and the instructor

- Tasks for becoming familiar with introductory course materials and the technology

This first phase of engagement is the time for the instructor to begin the process of creating a sense of presence and community. Mutual respect and the establishment of a safe environment for all participants will foster an energetic exchange of ideas that will increase as each phase is implemented. Activities in this phase also help students new to online learning become familiar with using technology to communicate. Plan an icebreaker carefully, as it sets the tone for future communications in the learning community. Table 5.1 lists elements to consider when designing a Phase 1 activity. Table 5.2 lists the activities contained in this chapter.

Table 5.1. Checklist for an Effective Phase 1 Activity

	Yes	No	Comments
1. Is the activity fun and nonthreatening?			
2. Is it person-focused (a social icebreaker)?			
3. Is it content-focused (a cognitive icebreaker)?			
4. Does it require learners to read one another's entries and respond to one another?			
5. Does it require the learner to find something in common with at least 10 percent of the learning community?			
6. Does it require a person to be imaginative or express genuine emotions or openness?			

Source: Adapted from *Engaging the Online Learner: Activities and Resources for Creative Instruction,* by R. M. Conrad and J. A. Donaldson, 2004, 2011, Jossey-Bass.

Table 5.2. Phase 1 Activities to Try

Activity	Type	Purpose
Ten-Question Hunt	Cognitive icebreaker	To orient the students to class setup and where to find information
Bucket List	Social icebreaker	To help students learn about one another's lifelong aspirations
Dream Job	Cognitive icebreaker	To envision a career once the student completes the course or program
E.T., Phone Home	Cognitive icebreaker	To welcome students to the class and obtain cognitive icebreaker-type information
Four Nouns	Social icebreaker	To familiarize students with each other and with using the learning management system to converse and interact with each other
Hot Potato	Social icebreaker	To encourage interaction between students while learning about each others' abilities and ways of thinking
Life Without . . .	Cognitive icebreaker	To urge learners to think critically about a course related topic
Location, Location, Location	Social icebreaker	To get students familiar with each other and comfortable using course discussion technology
Movie or Song of Your Life	Social icebreaker	To introduce class members through self-reflection
Passion	Social or cognitive icebreaker	To discuss what drives each person personally or academically
Rainbow	Social icebreaker	To learn how others view themselves from a visual perspective
Untidy Timeline	Cognitive icebreaker	To come to consensus about important key points
Would You Rather . . . ?	Social icebreaker	To allow students to familiarize themselves with each other and some of the web conferencing tools

TEN-QUESTION HUNT

Task: Students answer ten introductory questions about the course

Objective: To orient the students to the class setup and where to find information

Author: James C. Funk, Esq., COI, Marion Technical College, funkj@mtc.edu

Instructions

Ten questions are posed in an introductory e-mail—questions such as, Where is the syllabus located? Where are the worksheets located? When are assignments due? I ask students to reply to me via e-mail with the subject line "[Name] Answers to Questions." I award extra credit for completion of this assignment.

Activity Author's Note

I use this activity as a way to get students to look at posted documents that will have an impact on their completion of the course, such as grading rubrics, calendars, and course expectations, all of which can be posted in brief announcements. I respond directly to student e-mails; this gives me an opportunity to provide personal feedback at the beginning of the course. I always include a reminder that this is a college course and that they are not texting a friend or posting a tweet or a comment on Facebook. This is my introduction to the course. My first discussion thread asks them to introduce themselves and provide, at least, their major and their online experience. I do the first introduction. In addition, I make a point of responding to every introduction with a welcoming post and, perhaps, a follow-up question.

Book Authors' Note

This is a nonthreatening initial task to encourage student communication with the instructor and their understanding of some of the basic mechanics of the course.

BUCKET LIST

Task: To share lifelong aspirations and dreams

Objective: To envision learners' lives beyond the course content

Author: Rita-Marie Conrad, PhD, Institute for Educational Excellence, Duke University School of Nursing, ritamarie.conrad@duke.edu

Instructions

In the 2007 movie *The Bucket List*, two terminally ill men take a road trip to accomplish the list of things they had always wanted to do in life before they died ("kicked the bucket"). What are the top five things on your list? Where would you like to live? Travel? Work? What would you like to do before you leave this earth?

Activity Author's Note

It's important that learners get to know the people behind the "name on the computer screen" in an online course. This activity is one way to get to know a person beyond their academic discussion comments.

DREAM JOB

Task: To share and discuss each student's future ideal job

Objective: To identify and share future plans once the student completes the program

Author: J. Ana Donaldson, EdD, online educator and consultant, ana .donaldson@cfu.net

Instructions

It is often to our advantage to identify where we are headed in our future professional life. Your replies to the following questions may help you reflect on your goals for the future:

- Describe the ideal job that you hope to find yourself in down the road.
- Complete a search for a current job ad that closely matches your ideal position.
- Share the link to this ad and discuss what qualifications for the job you currently possess and those skills or experiences that you will need to obtain in the future.
- Discuss what skills or experiences might be added to your list at the completion of the current course (or program of study).

Activity Author's Note

Prior to starting the first class, one of my students found an ad for the job he wanted to be employed in at the end of his master's program. He taped the ad to the inside of his notebook for every class he attended. This strategy assisted him in ensuring that each step of his academic journey was taking him closer to his final goal. When he graduated, he was well prepared to start the job of his dreams.

E.T., PHONE HOME

Task: To connect with students via phone or Skype

Objective: To welcome students to the class and begin the process of building the learning community

Author: J. Ana Donaldson, EdD, online educator and consultant, ana .donaldson@cfu.net

Instructions

Once you have obtained a class roster that includes phone numbers or Skype identifiers, contact each student prior to the beginning of class or during the first week. Following are some suggested topics:

- Introduce yourself and why you are calling.
- Ask if the student has viewed the syllabus and obtained the necessary textbook or reference materials.
- Determine the technology available for student interaction.
- Discuss expectations from you and from the student.
- Encourage any questions or concerns that the student may have regarding the class.
- Conclude by reminding learners of your contact information and that you hope to talk with them again either via phone or online tools such as Skype in the days ahead.

You may want to conduct an additional call with each student later in the course as a checkpoint evaluation of how the course is going.

Activity Author's Note

This one-on-one interaction is important for establishing an atmosphere of encouragement and open communication. It helps create a clear sense of instructor presence.

FOUR NOUNS

Task: Introductory activity for the beginning of a course

Objective: To get students familiar with each other and comfortable using the learning management system (LMS) to converse and interact with each other

Author: Scott Fredrickson, PhD, University of Nebraska Kearney, fredricksons@unk.edu

Instructions

1. Select four nouns that you feel describe you well to your colleagues. In the Introduction forum, post a message with your name in the subject line. In the body of the message, list your four nouns.

2. Read the nouns other students have chosen.

3. By the third day of class, select three students who, if possible, have not had replies to their posting. Take two of the nouns and guess why that person might have chosen them. You may choose one student you know from other classes or elsewhere, but you must choose at least two students you have never interacted with before.

4. After at least three students have stated why you picked your nouns, provide your own reasons. Also reply to each response to your nouns with a comment about what you think of the reasoning the other students have used for your noun selection.

5. Respond to replies to any of your postings.

Activity Author's Note

I adjust the numbers on this activity depending on the number of students in the class. If I have a large class, I will reduce the numbers a bit, but with a smaller class, I increase them. I want at least three or four classmates responding to each student. I will also closely observe the threads as they are posted, and if too many students are selecting one student or someone is being left out, I will direct a particular student to reply (or not to reply) to a specific student. This activity gets folks fired up and talking. I make sure that the entire activity is completed the first week. If a student does not jump in right away (the first day) I contact him or her and gently get the process moving forward.

Book Authors' Note

A further way of defining the learning community during this first-week activity is to create a word cloud (at www.wordle.net, for example) of the chosen words. The common nouns between class members will be highlighted in the resulting image.

HOT POTATO

Task: Introductory exercise for an online course

Objective: To get students interacting while learning about each others' abilities and ways of thinking

Authors: Stephen Acheson, John Deere, AchesonStephenW@JohnDeere.com; Debrah Fordice, EdD, assistant professor, Luther College, fordde01 @luther.edu; and Cecilia Ruhlmann, John Deere Product Engineering Center, RuhlmannCeciliaM@JohnDeere.com

Instructions

Begin the activity by picking a topic from a menu of choices such as:

Au gratin potatoes: things that you think are cheesy

Whipped potatoes: things that make you feel a bit "whipped" or frazzled

Half-baked potatoes: things that drive you crazy

Tater tots: little things that mean a lot to you

Baked potatoes: projects that you have completed

Boiled potatoes: times you were in hot water

Sweet potatoes: nice things that you have done for others

Rotten potatoes: things that you dislike

Once the group chooses a topic, one person provides an example for that topic, and then they pass it to the next person. Each person in the group has to answer at least twice. As in the real game of Hot Potato, the group members are encouraged to pass it on as quickly as possible. If you have extra time during the discussion, the group may want to try another round with a different potato option.

Activity Authors' Note

This activity is intended to get the group talking, share their thoughts, and show other members how they think. The results help the group members to learn about each other, their experiences, and their abilities to handle pressure.

Book Authors' Note

The fun part of this activity is having the group determine the potato type. It works in a chat format, Skype-type interaction, or discussion thread. If it is done asynchronously, the time between postings should be clearly stated. If time is a factor, the instructor may want to speed up the process by choosing the "potato style."

LIFE WITHOUT . . .

Task: To discuss what life would be like without an element that we take for granted

Objective: To realize the importance of the course topic in practical terms

Author: Rita-Marie Conrad, PhD, Institute for Educational Excellence, Duke University School of Nursing, ritamarie.conrad@duke.edu

Instructions for Instructor

Select either one topic from the course or the general course topic and ask learners to discuss what life would be like without it. For example, if this is an introductory engineering course, ask learners to describe what life would be like without microwaves and how they think engineering contributed to the development of microwaves. If this is an introductory technology course, ask learners to describe what life would be like without smartphones.

Activity Author's Note

Often learners don't realize the importance of a course, particularly an introductory one. This icebreaker starts them thinking about the relevance of the content to their everyday lives.

LOCATION, LOCATION, LOCATION

Task: Introductory activity for the beginning of a course

Objective: To get students familiar with each other and comfortable using course discussion technology

Author: Scott Fredrickson, PhD, University of Nebraska Kearney, fredricksons@unk.edu

Instructions

1. In the Introduction forum, create a thread and list three places you have lived and what you loved most about living there. For students who have not lived in three places, provide the same information for the places you *have* lived.

2. In the same posting, after using the Internet to find at least one interesting fact about each location that you did not already know, identify three places you have not lived but believe you would like to reside. Explain why you think you would like to live there.

3. Read all the other threads and find at least four locations that you had not considered. Make comments, ask questions, and otherwise discuss the choices with the person who made them.

Activity Author's Note

I adjust the numbers for this activity depending on the number of students in the class. If I have a large class, I will reduce the numbers a bit, but with a smaller class, I increase them. I want at least three or four classmates responding to each student. I also closely observe the threads as they are posted, and if too many students are selecting one student or someone is being left out, I will direct a particular student to reply (or not to reply) to a specific student.

Book Authors' Note

A fun extra credit option is for students to visually represent the diverse locations by creating a map showing the towns and cities identified. The map can then be posted to the course website along with individual photos of students.

MOVIE OR SONG OF YOUR LIFE

Task: Introductory exercise for an online course

Objective: To introduce class members through self-reflection

Author: J. Ana Donaldson, EdD, online educator and consultant, ana
.donaldson@cfu.net

Instructions

Think about where you are in your life. What has brought you to this moment?
What challenges have you faced, or what questions do you have?

If you were to pick an existing movie that represents your life at this moment
in time, what would it be? Would the movie be science fiction, action, romance,
documentary, drama, mystery, or other? If you are convinced the movie has not
been made yet, who would you choose for the director and leading actor? What
would be the film's name? What would be the key scene that would win the Oscar?

If you choose a song, post a link to iTunes or another accessible site to hear
the song or read the lyrics.

Post your movie or song choice and an explanation of why it was chosen.
Respond to at least two other postings that interest you.

Activity Author's Note

This is a great way to understand how students view themselves. You may be
surprised by their choices, and you are urged to ask the students for comparative
examples from the movie and real life. A movie or iTunes playlist from the class
postings might be a fun way for students to get to know each other better over
the duration of the class.

PASSION

Task: To share what in life or in the course content is the learner's main interest

Objective: To learn what community members consider key to their life and/or learning

Author: Rita-Marie Conrad, PhD, Institute for Educational Excellence, Duke University School of Nursing, ritamarie.conrad@duke.edu

Instructions

What are you most passionate about in your life? In your career? In regard to the subject of this course? Quickly write a list of all your passions. Don't spend a lot of time thinking about them. Write what initially comes to mind.

Activity Author's Note

What we are passionate about in life, work, and learning defines who we are. Sharing this information with the learning community provides insights into an individual that a simple "What's your name and why are you here?" icebreaker does not.

RAINBOW

Task: To introduce members of the community

Objective: To learn how others view themselves from a visual perspective

Author: J. Ana Donaldson, EdD, online educator and consultant, ana
.donaldson@cfu.net

Instructions

Depending on our culture and life experiences, each of us views color from a different perspective. Think of how you view the color yellow. How would you explain the color yellow to someone who has been blind from birth? What characteristics or words would you use?

Now, from the full spectrum of colors, choose the color that most represents you at this point in time. Post the color chosen to the discussion board and your reasons for this choice. Also select the color that is most unlike you, with the reasons why. You will need to respond to one individual whose color choice is the same (or similar to yours) and another whose choice is most unlike you. Find what you may have in common with each person.

The important thing to remember during this activity and class is that a rainbow is composed of an array of hues. Each color has its place, and each contributes to the experience. Each of us brings a diversity of experiences to the class. Don't hesitate to explore our shared rainbow.

Activity Author's Note

This icebreaker encourages diversity. Valuing each voice in the online experience is critical for success. You might want to create a graphic of the rainbow represented by the class's choices.

UNTIDY TIMELINE

Task: To reflect upon the importance of building an online community

Objective: To come to consensus about important key points

Authors: Stephen Acheson, John Deere, AchesonStephenW@JohnDeere.com; Debrah Fordice, EdD, assistant professor, Luther College, fordde01@luther .edu; and Cecilia Ruhlmann, John Deere Product Engineering Center, RuhlmannCeciliaM@JohnDeere.com

Instructions

We have all been shaped by the events in our lives, both minor and defining moments. Our age and the stage of life we are in when these events occur red also make a difference in how they affect us. What some of us are afraid to do as adults, others of us may have done as children or adolescents (such as scuba diving or performing on stage).

List in random order five events that have happened in your life. You may choose fun, intriguing, and amazing events, or you may choose an everyday occurrence. The goal is to list the five events in random order and allow your teammates to attempt to recreate your timeline in the correct order of occurrence. Your timeline format could look something like this example:

#__ I went to Disneyworld.

#__ I flew to Italy—by myself.

#__ I had my first hospital stay (besides my birth).

#__ I went scuba diving for the first time.

#__ I cried when I saw *E.T.* at the movie theater.

After your teammates have all had a chance to recreate your timeline, give them the correct order of events with as much description as you deem necessary. Some discussion should occur to further clarify your chosen events and how they may have influenced your life. Teammates may want to explain why they arranged others' timelines as they did.

Activity Authors' Note

This is a great way for learners to gain a better understanding of their teammates and their histories.

Book Authors' Note

Another twist is to ask students to find someone in the discussion with at least two shared experiences. In Phase 2, it is then up to the pair to discover other things they may have in common.

WOULD YOU RATHER . . . ?

Task: Orientation activity for the beginning of a course

Objective: To allow students to familiarize themselves with each other and some of the web conferencing tools (such as Elluminate)

Author: Tonya B. Amankwatia, PhD, DeSales University, tonya@desales.edu

Student Instructions

View the whiteboard images and determine which one best represents your preferred reply to the question posed. Choose a pointer or text tool when directed and click the image of your choice. Observe how many people differ or share your choice and discuss your choice when directed. You may customize the shape and color of your tool if using a web application like Elluminate.

Instructor Instructions

Think of how you would want students to complete the following question: Which _____ would you rather be _____ right now? Some examples are vacation spot, visiting; country, visiting; dessert, enjoying; recreational activity, enjoying; world event, attending; color, wearing; and animal, holding. Using a PowerPoint slide, put the question in the title area. Then in the content area insert a table with two horizontal rows and two or three vertical columns. Locate four to six representative, copyright-compliant images that answer the question. Place each image in its own cell of the table. Repeat this process two more times for each new question. Ask the question verbally and then ask learners to choose a pointer device or the text tool to select the image indicating their answer. Provide an opportunity for learners to elaborate on their answers.

Activity Author's Note

In addition to giving us an opportunity to get to know each other, I have used this as a way to help familiarize learners with the Elluminate interface and the tools that they can use to share their input. Some of my images are purposely funny. During major events such as the Olympics, I've placed an image of the host country in a cell and let the learners explain why. This works well with groups of ten or less. I like the visual effect of the various insertion points of blinking stars, smiles, arrows, and such on the images. If you have a big group, people can choose a text color and place their first and last initials on an image.

Book Authors' Note

This activity works especially well in a hybrid setting where you can have the class working together in the first or second class meeting.

Phase 2 Activities: Communicate

The goal in Phase 2 of the Phases of Engagement model is to begin the process of developing trust and increasing interaction between students. By beginning interaction with just one other student, the learner is encouraged to share ideas and begin to explore the content of the course. Communication is the key word for this stage. Beginning to share ideas, discuss differing views, and arrive at a compromise on partner postings are key components of effective student engagement at this point in the course.

The activities included in this chapter encourage discussion between learners focusing on course content, with the element of consensus added to encourage a deeper sharing of ideas. A student's level of connection increases when she or he is asked to defend a personal perception or statement. The instructor should assign the student partners based on information from the Phase 1 icebreaker activity. The constructive expression of differing views is encouraged, with consensus being the outcome of many of the activities. A safe environment for engagement continues to be maintained, one interaction at a time. Table 6.1 lists elements to consider when designing a Phase 2 activity. Table 6.2 lists the activities contained in this chapter.

Table 6.1. Checklist for an Effective Phase 2 Activity

	Yes	No	Comments
1. Is the activity academically oriented?			
2. Is it content-focused?			
3. Does it require learners to read one another's entries?			
4. Does it require that peers express what they agreed with or liked about each other's work?			
5. Does it require that peers indicate how others' work could be improved?			
6. Have guidelines or a rubric been provided stating how learners should provide feedback to one another?			

Source: From *Engaging the Online Learner: Activities and Resources for Creative Instruction,* by R. M. Conrad and J. A. Donaldson, 2004, 2011, Jossey-Bass.

Table 6.2. Phase 2 Activities to Try

Activity	Type	Purpose
100 . . . 150	Partner consensus	Introductory task for partner consensus about important key points
Five Words	Partner discussion	To identify and share students' expectations of the course
Boolean Search	Tool familiarity	To develop student Internet skills using Boolean operators
Elevator Talk	Partner consensus	To come to consensus about important key points
Focused Listening	Expectations of students	To develop skills needed by effective listeners
Let's Explore Lingo	Partner discussion	To work with a partner to search the Internet and then use common lingo and terminology
Online Resource Time Travel	Tool familiarity	To develop an informed appreciation of the university's online library services using a wiki as a method for synthesizing and integrating information and ideas
Reading a Brief	Cognitive strategy	To teach critical thinking skills in evaluating materials read
Reincarnation	Partner discussion	To learn about the field's leaders and discuss with a partner
Uh-Oh!	Partner discussion	To reflect on aspects of the course that are not clear

100 . . . 150

Task: To reflect upon the importance of building an online community

Objective: To come to consensus about important key points

Authors: Stephen Acheson, John Deere, AchesonStephenW@JohnDeere.com; Debrah Fordice, EdD, assistant professor, Luther College, fordde01@luther.edu; and Cecilia Ruhlmann, John Deere Product Engineering Center, RuhlmannCeciliaM@JohnDeere.com

Instructions

1. Each person should write one hundred words on a key point from the current week's discussion. An example prompt is "why building community in an online environment is important."

2. Once each partner has written their one hundred words, pairs of students should combine their reflections into a 150-word paper synthesizing the points the dyad feels are most important in building an online community.

Book Authors' Note

This activity helps students determine their individual beliefs on a topic and then work with one other to collaboratively document the pair's consensus. The interaction within the dyad in questioning and being willing to modify individual statements is the power of this task. The evolution of the final statement often involves a deeper individual reflection as each person rethinks his or her initial statement. If there is an impasse, the partners might find it beneficial to ask the other member to provide examples to support her or his statements. This is a case where concrete examples provide clarification for broad generalized statements.

FIVE WORDS

Task: To share and discuss each student's course expectations

Objective: To identify and share students' expectations of the course

Author: J. Ana Donaldson, EdD, online educator and consultant, ana
.donaldson@cfu.net

Instructions

You have now had some time to review the course syllabus and objectives. What
are your expectations for this course? Use the following guidelines to describe
and share what you see ahead of you for the class:

- What experiences would you like to have in the course?
- What practical lessons do you expect to learn in this course?
- How do you expect to meet the learning objectives stated in the syllabus?
- What strategies will you use to determine whether you have met the course
objectives?
- Describe the experiences you bring to the course that might enrich the discussion and advance your own learning process.
- Share your responses with your assigned partner.

Now the fun part begins. You will need to work with your partner to agree
upon the five words that describe your shared expectations. Post your final five
words in the subject line of the assigned discussion thread. Identify and post each
of your responses in the same posting in the body of the discussion posting.

Activity Author's Note

This is a great activity for use early in the semester to ensure that expectations
are realistic and based on the syllabus, instructor introductions, and preliminary
readings. If some students are veering in the wrong direction or have chosen to
ignore the documented information, you should contact these individuals. It is
much easier to correct this problem in Phase 2 and not wait until the posting of
final grades.

BOOLEAN SEARCH

Task: To complete an Internet exploration of course concepts or terms

Objective: To develop student Internet skills using Boolean operators

Authors: Roger Baker, learning consultant, CUNA Mutual Group, Roger .Baker@cunamutual.com; and David Graw, grawdave@gmail.com

Instructions

Prior to this activity, students receive instruction about Boolean operators and are given an opportunity to practice their search skills. Then students are given a random list of seven terms that they will have to find using various Internet searches. Students are required to define the terms and provide documented evidence of their hunt. Students who provide the most complete and accurate documentation will be considered successful scavenger hunters. Following are terms used in an introduction to distance education course:

1. Computer-mediated communication
2. Asynchronous learning
3. Synchronous learning
4. Podcasting
5. Webcasting
6. Media streaming
7. VoIP

Book Authors' Note

Students may be familiar with Internet searching, but may not understand the power of Boolean logic. There are many resources on the web regarding this search option. Be sure to provide a link to an explanation along with the activity description. Each course will use a separate list of terms. It is beneficial to post the best responses in the course for future student reference. This activity is not supported by the Google search engine.

ELEVATOR TALK

Task: To discuss and create a brief description of an assigned concept

Objective: To come to consensus about important key points

Author: J. Ana Donaldson, EdD, online educator and consultant, ana .donaldson@cfu.net

Instructions

If you had only the length of time it took to ride several floors in an elevator with a stranger, what would you say as a summary of the assigned readings for this module? Post your description to the assigned area. Your task is to work with your partner and their posted description to come to consensus on your "talk." Post the final agreed-upon "elevator talk" to the assigned area with a title for the final posting. If there is any doubt about your final description, it is advised that you find a tall building and a willing stranger.

Activity Author's Note

This is an amusing way for students to begin working with a partner and discussing key concepts from the assigned readings. The role of the instructor in Phase 2 is to make sure that the activity represents a contribution from each partner. You will need to monitor the activity discussion and provide guidance to ensure a collaborative effort.

FOCUSED LISTENING

Task: To develop a deeper understanding of learning

Objective: To develop skills needed by effective listeners

Author: J. Ana Donaldson, EdD, online educator and consultant, ana .donaldson@cfu.net

Instructions

In an online setting, understanding of the material is often based on the number of pages read or the number of video lectures viewed. Even in everyday conversations, the listener is often more focused on their own response than the other individual's contribution. The concept of "active listening" is that you are focused on what the individual is going to say next and not on your own response. This effective approach can be encouraged for online discussions.

In the presentation format of new material, it is also important to listen for key elements. One way to accomplish this is to consider the four-question methodology. As you read the required material (or view the lecture), concentrate on the question you have been assigned. After you have completed the reading, discuss your thoughts with your peer partner, come to consensus, and post your items to the assigned discussion thread. Read the other responses to your post and comment on at least one other response. Also review the other threads and see if you can add to their discussion. Extra credit is available if you have meaningful responses to each of the four threaded discussions.

1. What do you agree with?

2. What are the major concepts?

3. What questions do you still have?

4. What are examples that support what was presented?

Activity Author's Note

It is important for students to understand that learning happens at a deeper level than simply getting through the assigned number of pages. This task requires students to form their own opinions and share their experiences. You may want to vary your list of four questions to fit the topic; for question number 3, I have substituted "What don't you agree with or find as a new concept?"

LET'S EXPLORE LINGO

Task: To learn useful messaging terms

Objective: To work with a partner to search the Internet and then use common lingo

Authors: Paula Schmidt, EdD, Clarke University, paula.schmidt@clarke.edu; Antoinette Givens, antoinettegivens@hotmail.com; Peggy Fortsch, EdD, Allen College, fortscps@ihs.org

Instructions

When posting messages on a discussion board or in a chat, people often convey thoughts, emotions, and expressions using various combinations of letters, numbers, and symbols. To someone unfamiliar with online terminology, this "lingo" may seem meaningless, but if you don't know what it is you could be missing a lot, JTLYK!!

Use whatever resources are available to you to decode the following online lingo. Your challenge is to add an additional five terms to the chart. Be sure that the terms are inoffensive enough to be shared with your grandmother. After you have had a chance to discover the lingo, set up a chat time with your partner to practice your new terminology, plus any new terminology you may learn in your searching.

Lingo Chart

Symbol	What It Means	Symbol	What It Means
:{		MTF	
:O		OIS	
;-)		OTP	
AFAIK		ROFL	
BBIAF		SITD	
BFN		SO	
BRB		SYS	
BRBK		TX	
BSY		TY	
CID		TYVM	
HTH		1.	
IGP		2.	
JTLYK		3.	
kk		4.	
LOL		5.	

Book Authors' Note

Since some commonly used abbreviations contain questionable language, the note about the chosen five terms being acceptable for grandmothers is a lesson that we learned the hard way. This task is a way to have the partner group work together on their communication and Internet search skills.

ONLINE RESOURCE TIME TRAVEL

Task: To take part in an imaginary time-traveling troupe that explores university online library services and to bring back new information and insights to share with their younger selves using a wiki

Objective: To develop an informed appreciation of the university's online library services using a wiki as a method for synthesizing and integrating information and ideas while interacting constructively with classmates

Author: Cindy Officer, doctoral candidate, Gallaudet University, cindy.officer @gallaudet.edu

Instructions for Students

For this activity, we are going to forge a time-traveling navigation team. Each of us will explore and chart the university's online library services with the intention of bringing this information back to the current year to share with our younger selves. As a team, we will create a wiki *[insert definition of a wiki]*. Please go to *[online library site]* to begin exploring their services. Make notes of exciting findings that your younger self would appreciate. A wiki has been started at *[link]*. Read the initial posting, the postings of your teammates, and then add your posting. Explain how and why discoveries from the library will benefit your younger self. Use creative and constructive language when addressing your younger self and classmates. (Imagine how you would feel being addressed by an older version of yourself.) Please be sure you've read previous postings, and contribute new insights.

Instructions for the Instructor

The instructor should become thoroughly acquainted with the university's online library (possibly with assistance from a librarian). The instructor needs to draft the initial wiki in a manner that incites further exploration of the library, perhaps by asking open-ended questions.

Activity Author's Note

The overall takeaway from this activity has been described, for the most part, as wonderful. Learners who are new to online classes often revel in how convenient and resourceful their online library is. Like its physical counterpart, the online library takes some wandering through to discover the wealth of information it contains, and this activity propels students through the online library. Learners often comment that they expect the library to become a frequently used tool in their online repository. The downside of this activity has some learners expressing a dislike of the wiki method. (One learner described it as arriving late to an Easter egg hunt with most of the goodies already "claimed.")

Book Authors' Note

This activity can be expanded to include any online service that needs to be explored by the students to understand its relevance and available resources.

READING A BRIEF

Task: To effectively understand and document the course reading assignments

Objective: To learn critical thinking skills in evaluating materials read

Author: Mary Herring, PhD, University of Northern Iowa, mary.herring @uni.edu

Instructions

You will be required to write a brief paper (one to three pages long) about your thoughts, reactions, questions, and ideas regarding the weekly reading assignments. The answers should include information from the assigned chapters. These briefs will form the basis of discussions and will help you to chart your own intellectual process. You should structure your comments using the question numbers. Grammar and spelling will be checked on these papers. You can redo one of the three briefs that receives less than a perfect score. You will have *two* weeks after the paper is returned for the redo.

Guidelines for Writing a Brief

1. Read the assigned chapter(s).

2. Underline or take notes as you read.

3. Create an outline of the author's discussion. This will force you to sort out major points from supporting examples, background, context, and so on.

4. Respond to the article. What did you make of it? Do you agree? Do you find the evidence compelling? What did it make you think about? What might be the most important implications of this discussion? Why is it important?

5. Write up the brief. The outline of the chapters should be reported separately by textbook. The responses for the four assigned reading brief questions should address both chapters.

How Do You Write the Brief?

1. You have a one- to three-page limit. If your brief extends to page three, you must edit—and not by reducing the type size or decreasing the width of the margins.

2. Budget your space wisely. The purpose is not to reiterate the article, but to analyze it.

3. Writing mechanics are very important. Follow the rules of good grammar and style. Follow the APA bibliographic form.

4. Proofread, and then proofread again.

5. Do not use a cover page. Put your name, your course number, the date, and the module number in the upper right-hand corner of the first page. You may also use a title if you choose.

6. Exchange papers with your peer partner and, per the rubric, provide feedback to one another. Use that feedback to improve your paper before turning it in to me.

Questions to Be Addressed in Each Brief

1. What new insights did you gain from this reading?

2. What questions did the author raise for you about:
   - Learning online?
   - Designing for online instruction?
   - Society?
   - Technology?

3. What are the practical and applicable implications of this author's work for designing online instruction?

4. How does this author's view compare to your own? Explain your response.

Activity Author's Note

The questions to be addressed in item 2 will change depending on the content of the course. It is important that the topics be broad enough that they will relate to each chapter read over the course of the class. This breadth helps students consider how each reading assignment addresses the topics emphasized in the course.

Book Authors' Note

This activity provides learners with a framework that generates a much deeper level of discussion and synthesis than otherwise occurs. It is particularly helpful with learners who are new to interacting online.

REINCARNATION

Task: Introductory dyad

Objective: To learn about the field's leaders and discuss them with a partner

Author: J. Ana Donaldson, EdD, online educator and consultant, ana .donaldson@cfu.net

Instructions

Every professional field is directed by the scholars and leaders who have gone before.

Reflect on the individuals you consider influential in our field of study. Pick three individuals who have made a lasting impact, living or deceased. Create a grid of at least three contributions that each individual has made to our field, with at least three additional references to publications by or about the individual. As you review your grid and personal readings, which individual would you like to be if reincarnation or cloning were an option?

Post your choice, a 250-word explanation for the choice, and your grid. Also include why the other individuals were not chosen. Remember to respond to your partner's posting about the choices and what you learned about the field's leaders.

Submission Template

Choice: *[name of scholar or leader]*

Explanation for choice: 250 words to justify choice or nonchoice with references to the grid

Following is a sample grid.

Individual	3+ Contributions	3+ References (APA)
1	1	(reference 1)
	2	(reference 2)
	3	(reference 3)
2	1	(reference 1)
	2	(reference 2)
	3	(reference 3)
3	1	(reference 1)
	2	(reference 2)
	3	(reference 3)

Activity Author's Note

This is a great way for individuals new to a field to define the leaders in the profession. By doing this activity with a partner, students can learn that it is acceptable to have different ideas and that there is something to be learned from each other. This task can also result in a class-generated list of leaders and a reference list. It is the instructor's job to make sure that any missing names are added.

UH-OH!

Task: To discuss aspects of any course content that needs clarification

Objective: To clarify aspects of course content that need further processing by learners

Author: Rita-Marie Conrad, PhD, Institute for Educational Excellence, Duke University School of Nursing, ritamarie.conrad@duke.edu

Instructions

Now that you are nearing the end of this *[discussion, module, unit, or activity]*, which aspect(s) of the content still seem "fuzzy" or unclear in your mind? Discuss these aspects with your colleague, determine which ones you can explain to one another, post one to three of the "uh-ohs" that both of you need clarification on, and e-mail them to me *[the instructor]*.

Activity Author's Note

This activity is based on the Aha! reflective activity in our first book, *Engaging the Online Learner.* In that activity, learners are asked to share moments of "unexpected clarity" with the content. The Uh-Oh activity is the antithesis of this clarity and ideally leads to Aha! moments. The reason I have learners e-mail these to me is that sometimes they are embarrassed about not understanding something. If they communicate this in a private e-mail, I can then take the entire class list of "uh-ohs" and address my answers in a synthesized document to the entire class as part of an FAQ (frequently asked questions) posting.

Phase 3 Activities: Collaborate

The third phase of the five Phases of Engagement is the time many instructors begin course interaction. Without traversing the first two stages, the interaction between students usually remains at the communication level and never truly reaches the goal of effective collaboration. It is when students are actively interchanging ideas and are working toward collaboratively solving course-related tasks that the benefits of the online learning experience are realized.

Phase 3 types of assignments normally focus on group projects and discussions with supportive rubrics for assessment. The results of the collaborative projects should represent authentic tasks that can be implemented beyond the end of the course. Previous team projects or activities that demonstrate the attainment of course objectives can also be adapted to the online setting from the classroom. The activities in this chapter range from introductory activities to strengthen the team-building aspect of Phase 3 to team discussions and collaborative tasks. Table 7.1 lists elements to consider when designing a Phase 3 activity. Table 7.2 lists activities contained in this chapter.

Table 7.1. Checklist for an Effective Phase 3 Activity

	Yes	No	Comments
1. Does the activity consist of more than just questions and answers?			
2. Is it content-focused?			
3. Is the activity authentic? Does the activity have value beyond the learning setting?			
4. Does it require learners to work collaboratively and use their experiences as a starting point?			
5. Does it require team members to demonstrate critical thinking?			
6. Is the team required to produce a synthesized response or end product?			
7. Does the activity build skills that can be used beyond the length of the course?			
8. Are team members held individually accountable for their contributions to the activity?			

Source: Adapted from *Engaging the Online Learner: Activities and Resources for Creative Instruction,* by R. M. Conrad and J. A. Donaldson, 2004, 2011, Jossey-Bass.

Table 7.2. Phase 3 Activities to Try

Activity	Type	Purpose
Build Your Own Search Engine	Team-generated resource tool	To generate a student-driven search tool of course content using Google Custom Search Engine with researched material and core course content
Building a Better Keyboard	Team problem solving	To work collaboratively to analyze and design a new concept
Group Wiki	Team discussion	To identify and effectively communicate the relevance of the chosen topic
Hot Air Balloon	Determining individual characteristics for group assignments	To provide a fun and reflective way to identify a student's interests and strengths to others in the class
Reverse Brainstorm	Team discussion	To determine how to improve collaboration and teamwork
Student-Powered Ning Blogging	Team discussion with increased diversity of perspectives	To share each others' perspectives on common readings while gaining the opportunity to "face off" in collegial ways
Team Kickoff	Instructor-led team meeting	To initially organize the team
Vegetables	Introduction for new team members	To begin to create a learning community and introduce learners to each other in a fun, interactive fashion
Virtual Lounge	Collaborative discussion for individual writing task	To allow students to discuss with their peers aspects of a comparison essay
Vlogs Are Us	Group building content	To process content through learner-led discussions
Whine and Cheese Party	Midcourse interaction	To provide a midcourse discussion to encourage community interaction

BUILD YOUR OWN SEARCH ENGINE

Task: Students-build a search engine to extend course content, practice, and understanding

Objective: To generate a student-driven search tool of course content using Google Custom Search Engine with researched material and core course content

Author: Kathleen Gradel, EdD, professor, SUNY Fredonia, gradel@fredonia.edu

Instructions for Students

There are two roles in this activity: producer and consumer. For each topic, there are two producers. All other students are consumers for that topic. Producers sign up to host a topic of their choice. Consumers are expected to participate in all.

Hosts' jobs are to do the following after the published posting timeline:

1. Read or review the assigned article(s) or media.

2. Sign up for the content that you wish to lead.

3. With your partner, compile four big-idea questions about your content that will push consumers beyond the lowest level of Bloom's Taxonomy (do not post a "remembering" or straight fact question). Build the questions into a table format in a posted shared-document format that consumers can make a copy of and then use for their own inputs; this will be your Q&A format.

4. Research the responses to your questions, locating valid web resources that augment what the text has given you as background. While you do this, (a) create an answer key for your Q&A format and (b) keep track of which keywords work and which keywords *do not* work. *Note:* You are not trying to locate generic sources of information or compile a massive list of resources for others to explore.

5. Once you have isolated a few solid, valid web resources, build a Custom Google Search Engine that contains *only the websites that you have selected* as the optimal places to go to get the answers to your questions. Ensure that you add info as you build it about the keywords that your colleagues should use in their search. Note the following resources:

   • Google's step-by-step instructions, plus all that's fit to print: http://code.google.com/intl/en/apis/customsearch/docs/start.html

- Movie tutorial: http://www.butterscotch.com/tutorial/Custom-Search -Engines-Using-Google-Custom-Search
- To make your own custom search engine, start here: http://www.google .com/cse

When you are finished, you can go back to your search engine link and click on the hyperlink to "manage your existing search engines." (The link is under the button that you clicked to create your search engine.)

6. Post your search engine, your Q&A format, and your Q&A format answer key URLs to our Google Doc tracker.

Consumers' jobs are to:

1. Read or review the assigned article(s) or media.

2. Use at least two teams' search engines and Q&A formats to strengthen your understanding of and fluency with the assigned material.

3. Check your own work against the Q&A format answer keys.

4. Take the module's online quiz.

Instructions for the Instructor

1. Identify the content that needs to be reviewed; post articles, links, and any other materials that may be needed.

2. Post directions for the assignment (including job descriptions), as well as the online posting requirements and mechanics. Add links to any tutorials that may be needed.

3. Set up the online venue where students will post their links. For example, I typically set up a Google Doc; this link is posted to the course wiki (but could be made available via the learning management system or another venue).

4. "Shadow" the process; guide students in timing, accuracy, and such as needed.

5. Post the "normal" assessment of the module's content.

6. Identify and clarify for students how this work factors into the grading system.

Activity Author's Note

This activity is another way of reviewing course content, with students doing the work and making meaning of it, while extending their own (and their colleagues' understanding) by using additional web resources, along with the Custom Google Search Engine tool. This activity replaces the standard discussion forum, blog, or study guide for providing additional practice with the material. It also puts the student in the driver's seat. I have used this as a way to create "living" study guides of text chapters, as well as other course content. The possibilities are nearly endless.

Examples are very helpful for prompting good work on this product. I recommend providing an example on topics that are different from what is assigned for this activity, to minimize duplication. I have students preview materials on Bloom's Taxonomy and practice building questions that get at different levels of critical thinking *before* they become hosts in this activity.

In addition to "standard" grading, instructors may want to embed both self- and other evaluation into the process. For example, I have students self-evaluate their product and their collaboration behaviors; then I ask partners to separately reflect on how the collaborative process worked in their own journals. You may also have students rate their favorite search engines and Q&A formats after they have used them. Instructors should monitor production, but not lead. It is important to value this work in the grading framework, since this is a way to track students' formative use of at least some of the course's readings and media.

Book Authors' Note

This is a great example of a collaborative effort for reviewing key concepts and learning new skills while taking understanding to a deeper level. Be aware that web addresses may change over time. It is recommended that you check each link prior to the assignment.

BUILDING A BETTER KEYBOARD

Task: To participate in a group creative problem-solving activity

Objective: To work collaboratively to analyze and design a new concept

Author: Sharon Smaldino, PhD, Northern Illinois University, ssmaldino @niu.edu

Instructions

As you read this, you are undoubtedly sitting at a keyboard. Look at it closely. This is most likely a QWERTY keyboard, called such because of the order of the first six keys of the top row. Why are the keys arranged in such a strange way? This design was created in the days of the typewriter. Is this design still necessary in the digital age? Is there a better keyboard design?

In this activity, you will work with your group to discover why the keyboard is arranged in this manner. Then your group will design a new keyboard based on the changed needs of modern communication. Be creative with this activity, and question any assumptions you have about what a keyboard has to be. One member from each group will post the group's design and an explanation to the discussion board. Finally, each individual will comment on at least one other group's design and respond to comments about their own group's design.

Process

- Review the activity description with a focus on the group and individual grading rubrics.

- Divide the tasks according to your own group's method for collaboration. You'll want to do this through either the discussion board or the group e-mail option.

- Research the history of the keyboard, specifically the reasons for the QWERTY design. Write a few paragraphs explaining why this method was used and why it is obsolete. Post this in your group's discussion board.

- Using your group's experience and research (minimal research), brainstorm what your new keyboard will look like. The chat function on your group page would be an excellent way to do this and should only take fifteen or so minutes.

- Select one of your group's ideas, or combine several, to be your new keyboard design.

- Create a graphic representation of your new keyboard. Since no one is an ergonomics expert, these designs are not expected to be perfect. In fact, the more creative your design, the better.

- Write a few paragraphs explaining why your group designed the keyboard in this way. Include a brief description of traditional education methods that may need to be adapted for distance education settings.

- Post your design and the explanations to the main discussion board. Only one group member needs to do this for the entire group. The explanation should be in the main body of the post, and the design should be an attachment to the post.

- Individually, read and comment on at least one other group's keyboard.

- As a group, respond to comments and questions from your classmates about your group's design.

Evaluation

The group task is worth twenty-five points. The individual response is worth ten points. Rubrics for both assignments appear next.

Group Task Rubric	
Meets	*Does Not Meet*
Labor is divided equitably among group members; everyone participates (5 points)	Labor is unequally divided; one or more individuals do the bulk of the work (0 points)
History paper accurately describes the history of the QWERTY keyboard, is at least two paragraphs long, and has few or no grammatical or spelling errors (5 points)	History paper is inaccurate, fewer than two paragraphs long, and has many grammatical and spelling errors (0 points)
Keyboard design is innovative and clearly represented using a graphic (10 points)	Keyboard design is identical to the current design, or the graphic representation of the design is difficult to comprehend (0 points)
	Continued

Group Task Rubric

Meets	Does Not Meet
Explanation paper describes the rationale for the keyboard design, is at least two paragraphs long, and has few or no grammatical or spelling errors (5 points)	Explanation paper does not describe the rationale for the keyboard design, is fewer than two paragraphs long, and has many grammatical and spelling errors (0 points)

Individual Response Rubric

Meets	Does Not Meet
Individual responds to one posting by another group (5 points)	Individual responds to his or her own group or does not respond (0 points)
Individual response reflects a substantial addition to the discussion (5 points)	Individual response does not reflect a substantial addition to the discussion and consists only of comments like "good comment" or "I agree" (0 points)

Conclusion

As technology changed, the demands on the technology changed, as well. The QWERTY keyboard was developed to fulfill a technological need. However, those reasons may no longer be valid. The same is true of education. As the technology available for distance education evolves, the methods must evolve as well. Traditional classroom methods are not necessarily appropriate for distance education. As you begin to develop instructional plans for distance education, make certain you question the usual ways before transferring them into distance education.

Book Authors' Note

This activity was designed for a class with a focus on distance education. It might also be adapted to question traditional concepts such as K–12 education, the classroom environment, or any other long-accepted concept or tradition.

GROUP WIKI

Task: Students report on and discuss various topics related to the chapters they are studying, as well as current events and topics of interest

Objective: To identify and effectively communicate the relevance of the chosen topic to your field of study and to the world around you

Author: Susan Mircovich, assistant professor of chemistry, Kenai Peninsula College, University of Alaska Anchorage, ifscm@kpc.alaska.edu

Instructions for Students

You will select or write your own topic during the first two weeks of class. I encourage you to work in groups, but you may work individually if you prefer. A maximum of four people may report on any one topic. See the discussion board for a sign-up list. You will be able to contribute to the wiki only for the topic you selected. You can use images or other media. It should be interesting and fun! You will also be required to comment on a minimum of two other topics or wikis during the semester. Following is the rubric (expectations) for reporting and commenting in our class wiki.

Wiki Rubric			
Unacceptable (0–27 points)	*Acceptable* (28–31 points)	*Good* (32–35 points)	*Excellent* (36–40 points)
No value or new information is added	Lacks two or three of the qualities for excellence	Lacks one or two of the criteria for excellence, but is well written	Accurate, original, relevant, well written, teaches; references are cited as appropriate

After each wiki due date, we can *all* see the wikis and comment on them. Have fun with your wiki! Click the Edit button to start your page. You can type, add pictures, links, audio, YouTube videos, and whatever you like. If more than one person is working on your topic, make sure that you are not going to report the same information. You can send them a message or divide up the topic right in your wiki page. I will make you an Elive session to enable you to work together if you like.

Guidance on the two comments you will make on your classmates' wikis follows (two posts are required, and each post is worth five points):

- Write down a few notes before typing your comment
- Reply in a way that shows your position
- Add to the discussion by critically reflecting on what is being discussed
- Move the discussion in a new direction or to a deeper level
- Ask a question to stimulate further thinking
- Communicate in a friendly, courteous manner
- Just saying "I agree" does not add to the discussion!

Source: Adapted from *Assessing the Online Learner: Resources and Strategies for Faculty,* by R. M. Palloff and K. Pratt, 2009, Jossey-Bass.

Instructions for the Instructor

First the instructor must create individual wikis for each topic and assign the students who signed up as editors of their respective wikis. Each week after the due date, the instructor reads the wiki submissions and grades them according to the rubric. In addition, submissions should be checked on a plagiarism-checking website or tool. The instructor provides each student with grading comments, plus comments on the wiki. The instructor opens up the wiki to allow the rest of the class to view and comment. The instructor should regularly grade comments according to the rubric requirements.

Activity Author's Note

This is a very interesting assignment for both students and instructors! I find that students are quite interested in reading what their classmates have written and are often surprised at what they have learned by writing their own wiki and reading their classmates' wikis. I believe that this assignment has been successful in helping students expand on what they have learned about course content each week.

Book Authors' Note

Wikis are a great learning tool for students. If you want to learn more about the use of wikis for online collaboration, see the book *Using Wikis for Online Collaboration: The Power of the Read-Write We,* by West and West (Jossey-Bass, 2009).

HOT AIR BALLOON

Task: Activity for team building

Objective: To provide a fun and reflective way to identify and share a student's interests and strengths with others in the class

Author: J. Ana Donaldson, EdD, online educator and consultant, ana.donaldson @cfu.net

Instructions

You are with a group of fellow students in a hot air balloon. The journey is delightful, until you notice that you are quickly descending for no apparent reason. Dangerous power lines are below the balloon, and quick action is necessary. One of you will need to be sacrificed over the side so that the rest will live.

Post to the activity discussion area why you should be chosen to survive. Your explanation should include what you can offer to the team as a project member. Remember—your life and the survival of the team will depend on the strength of the members chosen.

This activity is meant to be fun. No one will be harmed during, or as a result of, this task. Self-reflection is a part of this activity as you think of yourself as a team member and identify your future contributions to the completion of the final project for this course.

Activity Author's Note

This activity is particularly beneficial when you are determining the roles for a team. Leaders are quickly identified through their responses, as well as those with other skills. There is often a bonding experience demonstrated within the group as they negotiate for the saving of all members. My favorite posting was from an overachiever who went out on the Internet and gathered all the information available on hot air balloon repairs to ensure their inclusion.

REVERSE BRAINSTORM

Task: Using the reverse brainstorming strategy, analyze how your teamwork should function

Objective: To develop a team contract or improve teamwork

Author: Rita-Marie Conrad, PhD, Institute for Educational Excellence, Duke University School of Nursing, ritamarie.conrad@duke.edu

Instructions

Now that you have been assigned to collaborate as a team, it's important to determine how you will work together and avoid potential problems. Reverse brainstorming is a different way of looking at a problem. Unlike the use of brainstorming to find solutions, a reverse brainstorm looks at what might be causing the problem. In this case, I ask you to reverse-brainstorm the potential problem of "Our team is not working well." Brainstorm answers to the question, "How can we cause our team to not work well?" Use the answers to form a team contract that states how you all will avoid causing the team to function poorly. Sign and submit this contract in the course's dropbox.

Activity Author's Note

This activity can be introduced just after the group has been assigned. While the preceding instructions discuss forming a team contract, this activity can also be used as an opportunity to improve how the team is functioning after everyone has had an opportunity to work with each other for a few weeks. Depending on how well a team is working, you may wish to be present at this team discussion or ask for a summary of what the team plans to change.

STUDENT-POWERED NING BLOGGING

Task: Ongoing activity across the course to capture students' attention to and use of assigned readings and media and jointly publish

Objective: To share each others' perspectives on common readings while giving students the opportunity to "face off" in collegial ways with each other on hot-button topics

Authors: Kathleen Gradel, EdD, professor, SUNY Fredonia, gradel@fredonia .edu; Dani McKinney, PhD, assistant professor, SUNY Fredonia, Dani .McKinney@fredonia.edu

Instructions for Students

There are two "jobs" in this activity: participants and leaders. The leaders are the two blog hosts; the participants are discussants on the blog. Leaders sign up to host a topic of their choice; participants are expected to participate in all blogs.

Leaders' jobs are to do the following after the blog timeline cycle:

1. Read or review the assigned article(s) and media.

2. Create *one* discussion prompt or question *jointly* to get the discussion rolling on this topic by the set time or date.

3. Take turns responding to other students' posts that were posted by the assigned times during the module period, distributing "coverage" of the time period across the two leaders. Responses may do any of the following:

    • Ask the poster a relevant question

    • Point them to another person's comments

    • Reference them back to the article(s)

    • Give or ask for an example

    • Extend their thinking

    • Point to a supplementary (optional) reading

Participants' jobs are to do the following after the blog timeline cycle:

1. Read or review the assigned article(s) or media.

2. Using your thinking on the reading(s), post an initial post to the Ning blog to meet these expectations:

   • State your opinion clearly, with solid mechanics, including formatting.

   • Back up your response with a reference to something that we have used—or that you have located—to support your opinion.

   • Reference at least one prior comment that someone else on the blog has posted.

   • If you are referencing a web-based source of information, embed a working link to that source.

   • Sign your posting.

3. Later in the module, return to reply to at least one (a) response to your original post, and/or (b) another colleague's thinking.

Instructions for the Instructor

1. Choose and post articles (or other materials) that have multiple perspectives and are relevant to the content.

2. Post sign-ups for the term's discussion topics and roles.

3. Secure a free Ning (via Pearson for this example).

4. Set up the Ning (welcome posting).

5. Post directions for both leaders and participants for posting to the Ning.

6. Identify and publicize "jobs" for leaders and participants.

7. "Shadow" leaders, monitoring their posts; guide them in doing their hosting jobs as needed.

8. Identify and clarify for students how this work factors into the grading system.

9. Monitor discussions and pop in as relevant.

Activity Authors' Note

It is important for instructors to choose articles that have multiple perspectives and are relevant to the content. In our literacy technology course, for example, topics have included to Facebook with students or not and personal mobile tech in the classroom or not. Instructors should monitor discussions, but not lead. Since one of the goals is to foster students as discussion leaders, it is preferable to shadow leaders' blog hosting and guide them in the background (via e-mail or Skype, for example), empowering them to take the lead in the blogs. You should post directly only when such intervention is absolutely necessary. When posting sign-ups for the term's discussion topics and roles, we have used a GoogleDoc that is published front and center for students' access. It is also referenced in each of the module guides to remind students of expectations, timing, and the like. It is important to value this work in the grading framework, since this is a way to track students' formative use of at least some of the course's readings and media.

Book Authors' Note

As an online instructor, you should not hesitate to use emerging technology with your students. You can never be expected to know it all when it comes to technology. Often our students have become our instructors as we built our skills. It is important to remember that our students have already embraced social networking as a way of life. It is beneficial to incorporate this effective mode of communication and sharing into our classrooms.

TEAM KICKOFF

Task: To discuss the team function and activities

Objective: To organize the team

Author: Rita-Marie Conrad, PhD, Institute for Educational Excellence, Duke University School of Nursing, ritamarie.conrad@duke.edu

Instructions

Now that you've received your team assignments, I would like to meet with each team to discuss the required team activities and timeline. Please let me know when your entire team can meet with me via Skype. The meeting should take no more than an hour.

Activity Author's Note

This activity models how team meetings should work in the event that learners have never attended a meeting. You may wish to send out an agenda for it ahead of time. I require the entire team to be there before the meeting can begin, unless there is an emergency with one of the team members (but no more than one team member should be absent). This activity also ensures that I have all the learners' Skype login IDs, so that I can contact them as needed throughout the semester.

VEGETABLES

Task: Introductory exercise for the beginning of Phase 3

Objective: To begin to create a learning community and introduce learners to each other in a fun, interactive fashion.

Authors: Janine Kane, PhD, Loras College, Janine.Kane@loras.edu; Brenda Heitmeyer, Iowa Valley Community College, Brenda.Heitmeyer@iavalley.edu; Amy Renze, St. Anthony Hospital, ARenze@stanthonyhospital.com

Instructions

1. Please choose what kind of vegetable you would be—which one is most like you and why. Describe how the characteristics you share with this vegetable would affect your work on group activities both in traditional education and work settings, and in a distance education setting.

2. Find a picture of the vegetable you chose and include it in your response.

3. Post your responses on your group's activity discussion area.

4. Read the response of each member of your group. Post your individual reaction or response to the vegetables your group members chose.

Activity Authors' Note

Extra credit option. If you would like to earn extra credit on this activity, please list the vegetables described by all members of your group and find a recipe on the Internet that incorporates all of the veggies. Post the recipe's title and the web address where the recipe can be found.

Book Authors' Note

This is a fun and nonthreatening way for members new to the group to provide some insight into how they perceive themselves. The information to be shared goes beyond the usual introductory list of job title, number of children, and names of pets. This activity would also be appropriate for a Phase 1 icebreaker with students choosing a variety of "vegetable" responses to determine a recipe.

VIRTUAL LOUNGE

Task: To learn how to write a comparison essay

Objective: To allow students to discuss with their peers aspects of a comparison essay, thus applying what they've learned to their own comparison essay

Authors: Gina L. Hochhalter, instructor of English, gina.hochhalter@yahoo.com; Ricky Fuentes, Clovis Community College, Clovis, NM

Instructions for the Instructor

Students are asked to watch the ESL Miami Comparison Contrast video on YouTube at http://www.youtube.com/watch?v=3rNg17UhGr0. The video is embedded into the discussion followed by brief learning or discussion questions.

Instructions for Learners

Watch the ESL Miami Comparison Contrast video on YouTube at http://www.youtube.com/watch?v=3rNg17UhGr0. Note that at the halfway point of the video (2:08), the voice goes silent. This is so you can read the paragraphs. The voice-over will return.

Submittal instructions. The virtual lounge format is a discussion posting, which means that the conversation will go back and forth in writing. Your responsibility is to write in ways that will keep the conversation going. One technique for keeping the conversation moving forward is to write substantive replies to your classmates. Substantive replies are required for more than 50 percent of the points.

Virtual lounge postings can earn a maximum of twenty-five participation points. To receive the full participation points, you need to complete *both* of the following tasks:

1. Post one original response to the question in the posting instructions (ten points)

2. Reply substantively at least twice to a peer's posting (fifteen points). A substantive response should do the following things:

a. Summarize the writer's point you wish to respond to

b. Respond to it

c. Ask a question, so that the original writer or someone else can respond

Note: Not all responses have to be substantive; it's okay to reply casually to peers. But to receive full credit, at least two responses need to be substantive. Do not wait until the end of the time to post to the virtual lounge. Begin posting as soon as possible.

Grammar and sentence structure. Keep in mind that though the lounge is somewhat informal, your writing should be clear and meaningful. Please edit your writing, and please do not use text message jargon inappropriately in a virtual lounge posting.

Virtual Lounge Posting Instructions

Answer one to two of the following questions:

- How will the ESL Miami Comparison and Contrast video help you write your paper?
- What did you learn about writing a comparison and contrast paper from ESL Miami?
- What are the two subjects you're comparing in your essay?

Activity Authors' Note

Students really love to give their opinions about this video!

Book Authors' Note

It is critical that all students can access this YouTube video with audio capabilities. Be sure to check the link prior to the assignment.

VLOGS ARE US

Task: To facilitate discussion based on student-built collaborative vlogs as course content using VoiceThread and assigned course readings and media

Objective: To capture relevant big-idea questions about a chunk of course content

Author: Kathleen Gradel, EdD, professor, SUNY Fredonia, gradel@fredonia .edu

Instructions for Students

There are two roles in this activity: host and contributor. Within your team, there are one to two hosts for each VoiceThread. All others are contributors on that VoiceThread. Hosts sign up to host a topic of their choice. Contributors are expected to participate in all VoiceThreads.

The host's job is to do the following after the published posting timeline:

1. Read or review the assigned article(s) and media.

2. Sign up for the content that you wish to lead.

3. Create two different questions *jointly* to get the discussion rolling on this topic by the set time or date. With your partner, compile two big-idea questions about your content. Post the questions in two separate "frames" on your own VoiceThread. You may post a slide, image, video (through your own webcam, produced elsewhere, or linked to from another source).

4. Take turns responding to others' posts, distributing coverage of the time period across the two leaders. Responses may do any of the following:

   • Sandwich feedback

   • Answer or ask a relevant question

   • Point them to another person's comments

   • Reference them back to the readings or articles, guiding them to specific information

   • Give an example or ask them to provide a relevant example

   • Extend their thinking

   • Point to a supplementary (optional) reading

Participants' jobs are to do the following after the published posting timeline:

1. Read or review the assigned article(s) and media.

2. Using your thinking on the reading(s), post an initial post to one of the two questions on the VoiceThread to meet these expectations:

   - State your opinion clearly, with solid mechanics, including formatting.

   - Back up your response with a reference to something that we have used—or that you have located—to support your opinion.

   - Reference at least one prior comment that someone else has posted, if you are not the first poster.

   - If you are referencing a web-based source of information, give information on that source and the link.

   - Sign your posting by stating or typing your name.

3. Later in the module, return to the discussion and reply to at least one (a) response to your original post, and/or (b) another colleague's thinking.

Instructions for the Instructor

1. Identify the content that needs to be reviewed; it can be instructor-driven or student-driven.

2. Post articles, links, or other related materials if the content is instructor-driven, not student-researched.

3. Post directions for the assignment (including job descriptions), as well as the online posting requirements and mechanics. Add links to VoiceThread's excellent tutorials on how to do it.

4. Set up the online venue for students to post their VoiceThread links. For example, I typically set up a GoogleDoc that asks students to identify their name, topic, and VoiceThread URL. This GoogleDoc link is posted to the course wiki (but could be made available via the learning management system, for example).

5. "Shadow" the process, monitoring their posts; guide students as needed regarding timing, accuracy, and the like. In particular, provide backup coaching to hosts as they run into obstacles, need help with the material, or need help keeping the discussion focus on the topic.

6. Identify and clarify for students how this work factors into the grading system.

Activity Author's Note

I have used VoiceThread as the publishing platform because it allows either text or verbal contributions by participants, and hosts can use a variety of media for each question frame. In addition, it enables built-in video capture if any participant wants to be seen and heard. Further, there is a universal version that is screen reader-friendly.

This activity replaces the standard discussion forum or blog post as a mechanism for demonstrating understanding or application of the material. The host role also puts students in a pivotal facilitator role as coach or teacher or mentor, thus asking them to extend their own understanding of the material.

I have used this as a way to create "living" study guides of text chapters, as well as other course content. The possibilities are nearly endless. Examples are very helpful in prompting good work on this product. I recommend providing an example on topics that are different from the assignments for this activity, to minimize duplication. In some instances, I have had students preview materials on Bloom's Taxonomy and practice building questions that get at different levels of critical thinking *before* they become hosts in this activity.

In addition to standard grading, instructors may want to embed both self- and other evaluation into the process. For example, I have students self-evaluate their product and their collaboration behaviors; then I ask partners to separately reflect on how the collaborative process worked, in their own journals. You may also have students rate their favorite VoiceThreads, after they have participated in them. It is important to value this work in the grading framework, since this is a way to track students' formative use of at least some of the course's readings and media.

Instructors should monitor production, but not lead it.

Book Authors' Note

This is a great way to provide scaffolding for students as they learn to become effective facilitators. You can extend this activity to also use student video productions or even to capture virtual world scenarios (such as Second Life) to share with the groups.

WHINE AND CHEESE PARTY

Task: Midcourse class discussion or meeting

Objective: To provide a midcourse discussion to encourage community interaction

Author: J. Ana Donaldson, EdD, online educator and consultant, ana .donaldson@cfu.net

Instructions

Students are asked to meet in the conference or chat area of the class. They are asked to have their favorite snacks, cheeses, and crackers at hand. Some may choose to include an adult beverage. The students can use the first fifteen minutes of the session to vent about any issues outside of school that might be causing stress. It is important to steer the conversation away from problems within the course or with other students. Those sensitive topics should be dealt with directly with the instructor. Once the fifteen-minute timer dings, the class takes a collective breath and then proceeds with the topic of the call.

Activity Author's Note

Over the duration of a course, it is sometimes advantageous to provide a forum for interaction that is not graded or focused on academic concerns. Classes tend to have peaks and valleys. The difficult time in the Midwest is the month of February. We traditionally face weeks without sunlight, piles of dirty snow, and chilling temperatures. This situation is a perfect time for this type of activity. The downtimes in your own community might occur at different times in the year.

This activity can also be formatted as a popcorn and movie night. Every student starts by sharing their favorite movie while munching on popcorn or snacks. The purpose of this approach is to have a bit of fun and remind students that learning can also involve a sense of whimsy.

CHAPTER
8

Phase 4 Activities: Co-Facilitate

Co-facilitation is the target for the activities in this phase. Once the students find themselves in Phase 4, the instructor's role has transited to that of a fellow learner and resource for additional guidance, when needed. Each team is expected to be a co-facilitator of the remaining tasks for a final project or collaborative event that began in Phase 3. Students assume responsibility for their own learning at this stage of the course. Activities are marked by a high level of interaction and engagement.

The tasks in this chapter focus on a more advanced approach to group interaction and resource generation. More responsibility is given to the team members as they work together to reach common goals. The online role-play activity is a prime example of theory and content being creatively represented in the online setting. Several activities for Phase 4 might also be applicable during Phase 3, depending on the maturity of the learners and the level at which the course content is being understood. Table 8.1 lists elements to consider when designing a Phase 4 activity. Table 8.2 lists the activities contained in this chapter.

Table 8.1. Checklist for an Effective Phase 4 Activity

	Yes	No	Comments
1. Are the objectives for the activity clearly stated in the syllabus?			
2. Is there a rubric for the grading of the activity?			
3. Is the concept of a co-facilitated activity introduced at least two weeks before learners begin planning it?			
4. Are learners provided several weeks to plan the activity?			
5. Does the topic allow a person or team to be creative in their choice and implementation of the activity?			
6. Does the participation grade include participation in the co-facilitated activities?			

Source: Adapted from Engaging the Online Learner: Activities and Resources for Creative Instruction, by R. M. Conrad and J. A. Donaldson, 2004, 2011, Jossey-Bass.

Table 8.2. Phase 4 Activities to Try

Activity	Type	Purpose
Course Vocabulary Bank	Summative group task	To summarize core concepts in a collaborative vocabulary or term bank while encouraging students to use their own thinking, interpretation, and creativity
Facilitating Diversity Online	Team-created lesson plan	To design a lesson plan with activities for students that demonstrates diversity while facilitating learning online using interactive tools
Factoids	Collaboratively generated course resources	To summarize core concepts or "ahas" from course materials and use collaborative products to solve course problems (via case studies and discussions, for example)
Google Docs for Peer Evaluation	Team sharing evaluation tool	To conduct peer evaluation to improve student work, build community through peer evaluation, and assist the instructor in evaluation of student work
Online Role-Play	Group role-play	To guide knowledge attainment about a contemporary world problem that ends with the students studying, understanding, and representing one of the included perspectives
Virtual Dining Meeting	Inviting students to a chat	To set the stage for an introductory discussion for a virtual meeting

COURSE VOCABULARY BANK

Task: Student-driven generation of course content across the semester, using podcasting or other online tools

Objective: To summarize core concepts in a collaborative vocabulary or term bank while encouraging students to use their own thinking, interpretation, and creativity

Author: Kathleen Gradel, EdD, professor, SUNY Fredonia, gradel@fredonia.edu

Instructions for Students

1. Sign up for the term(s) that you wish to develop.

2. Read or review the related course materials.

3. Generate your own (not borrowed) definition of the term. Then explain how it can be used in a real content-relevant example. Next, provide a source of information for someone else to extend their understanding of the term.

4. Post your vocabulary entry to the course's online Vocabulary Bank and make sure you sign your posting.

Instructions for the Instructor

1. Identify the terms and/or ask students to generate terms from various chunks of course content. For example, I use a GoogleDoc that has some suggested terms. I ask students to add to my initial list.

2. Set up a way for students to sign up to do their work on the term(s). For example, I use a GoogleDoc for this.

3. Decide on the single or multiple types of media for students to use. For example, I have used all the following types over the years, choosing *one* of the following platforms for a particular group of students or term: (a) a GoogleDoc set up as a table; (b) GoogleDoc slides; (c) direct posting to wiki pages; (d) podcasting (for example, using computer-generated files such as with Audacity, using web-based podcasting venues, and/or mobile apps); (e) Glogster; and (f) pencasts.

4. Provide links to tutorials for students to gear up on the tech demands of the task.

5. Set up a collection point for all URLs if you are using tools that separately generate a unique URL.

6. Post directions for the assignment.

7. "Shadow" the process, monitoring students' posts; guide students in timing, accuracy, and such as needed.

8. Identify how this work factors into the grading system and clarify this process for students.

9. If possible, build in plans to use the Vocabulary Bank for other course activities (for test review and other assignments and discussions, for example).

Activity Author's Note

Asking students to do this activity reinforces their understanding of concepts and terms. It also can alleviate the confusion that many students have with new material when they feel "boggled" by the vocabulary. Producing a community- or course-specific Vocabulary Bank can also serve to address students' diverse learning needs and comfort zones.

I have used various media for this activity; instructors will want to choose the publishing platform(s) according to one or more of the following variables: (a) reinforcement of other tech use in the course; and/or (b) extension of students' use of technology tools; and/or (c) highest comfort level for the instructor to facilitate.

I have been able to use Vocabulary Banks generated from one class with a subsequent class and then have asked the subsequent class to build additional terms into the already started bank. This also gives the later students a ready-made set of resources as they gear up in the course. Examples are very helpful in prompting good work.

It is important to value this work in the grading framework, since this is a way to track students' formative uses of at least some of the course's readings and media.

Book Authors' Note

This is a great way to reinforce the important concepts within the course content. Asking students to generate postings using alternative technologies adds an opportunity for enhancing skills while addressing the needs of our visual or auditory learners.

FACILITATING DIVERSITY ONLINE

Task: To create an online lesson plan demonstrating diversity in students' content areas

Objective: To design a lesson plan with activities for students that demonstrates diversity while facilitating learning online using interactive tools

Author: Peggy A. Lumpkin, PhD, Georgia State University, plumpkin@earthlink .net

Instructions

The goal of this activity is to give you an opportunity to use the tools you have already encountered in this class to design an online section or module that you might create for your current or future students. Read through the following resource, which contains a quick course for educators who are preparing to teach either online or blended courses:

> Carr, T., Jaffer, S., & Smuts, J. (2009). *Facilitating online: A course leaders guide.* Cape Town, South Africa: Centre for Educational Technology, University of Cape Town.

After reading the guidelines, focus on Appendixes 5 (Course Principles) and 8 (Why Diversity Matters). Then post in your blog (or WebQuest or wiki) how you would create an online activity dealing with diversity and provide examples and artifacts. Feel free to add graphics, pictures, and appropriate links for your students. Post your completed work in the assignment dropbox provided.

Instructions for the Instructor

Select a resource guide on facilitating teaching online, or use the one mentioned above.

Participants will use an online interactive tool of their choice (such as a blog, WebQuest, or wiki) to design an online classroom exercise that demonstrates diversity in their content area.

Instruct students to read through the resource. Ask them to reflect on how the strategies suggested in the resource guide compare with those used in the online course they are currently taking.

An additional step includes having the participants share their reflections on a discussion board. After they read the guidelines, have the participants focus on Appendixes 5 (Course Principles) and 8 (Why Diversity Matters). Then instruct participants to either blog, design a WebQuest, or create a wiki that features an online activity dealing with diversity. Encourage them to feel free to add graphics and appropriate links for your students. The participants submit their work in an assignment dropbox for grading.

Activity Author's Note

I used this exercise for a course focused on classroom technology integration for early childhood, pre-K, and elementary school students. Participants were excited to learn about technology standards and examples of technology use in the classroom with very young students. This exercise gave them the opportunity to demonstrate their new technology skills and showcase some of their ideas about teaching diversity. Some who were already involved in early childhood centers shared photos of some of their students depicting the reality of a diverse student population.

Book Authors' Note

This activity requires students to be already familiar with interactive tools such as blogs, WebQuests, and wikis. Also, encourage other students to respond to the posting. It is beneficial when the activities are actually implemented and the results are shared with the class.

FACTOIDS

Task: Student-built, collaborative Factoids as course content

Objective: To summarize core concepts or "ahas" from course materials and use collaborative products to solve course problems (via case studies and discussions, for example)

Authors: Kathleen Gradel, EdD, professor, SUNY Fredonia, gradel@fredonia .edu; Dani McKinney, PhD, assistant professor, SUNY Fredonia, Dani.McKinney@fredonia.edu

Instructions for Students

1. Read or review the assigned article(s) or media.

2. Complete your factoid on your topic, following your job description.

3. Publish your factoid to the course's online community venue.

4. As colleagues use the materials, respond to their questions and clarification requests using the course's publishing venue.

Instructions for the Instructor

1. Identify the content that needs to be reviewed; it can be instructor- or student-driven. Ensure that the expectations for the final product make sense for students to use later in the course with a subsequent activity.

2. Post articles, links, and any other materials if the content is instructor-driven, not student-researched.

3. Identify "job descriptions" for the collaborative work. Do not leave "jobs" to chance, as this encourages overachievers to do their thing and slackers to do theirs. We use templates and examples as well as written job descriptions to make this explicit.

4. Set up the online venue. For example, we typically set up a GoogleDoc using a template for each team and post the link to the course wiki. We have also used GoogleDoc slideshows, ZohoWriter, and ZohoShow.

5. Post directions and job descriptions for the assignment, along with the online posting requirements. Consider emphasizing how valuable the factoids will be for students' future use in the course.

6. "Shadow" the process, monitoring students' posts as needed and guiding them in timing, accuracy, and the like.

7. Identify and clarify for students how this work factors into the grading system.

Activity Authors' Note

The activity may be used at midcourse to focus students' attention on a "chunk" of assigned readings or media. These materials are then published by the team, making the product available for themselves and colleagues to use for a course activity that you assign later.

Also, this activity can be done using a variety of online platforms. For example, we have used ZohoWriter, Google Docs (document and presentation), blogs, and wikis. The important variable is that the factoid must not be submitted on a "one-way street" to the instructor; it gets published to the community. Note that the term *factoid* does not mean that the compilation should be simply a collection of facts.

To make use of the factoid product function, the instructor must create an authentic subsequent activity that students will be required to use later in the course. In other words, students are building a "secondary source." Its value needs to come into play through another course activity, and it should not be just "another assignment." For example, in our courses, the factoids become references for the whole class to use as they complete a major benchmark case study assignment. Alternatively, the subsequent work could be a discussion or a debate, for example. It is important to value this work in the grading framework, since this is a way to track students' formative use of at least some of the course's readings and media.

In addition to "standard" grading, instructors may want to embed both self- and other evaluation into the process. For example, we have students self-evaluate their product and their collaboration behaviors; then we ask partners to separately reflect on how the collaborative process worked in their own journals. You may also have students rate their favorite factoids after they have used them for the later benchmark assignment.

Book Authors' Note

Be sure to provide examples of the types of factoids you are expecting from the class. This activity builds upon the student products to expand the learning experience in subsequent tasks. The instructor needs to be an active participant through all phases of this activity and future applications.

GOOGLE DOCS FOR PEER EVALUATION

Task: To access Google Docs and use them as a formative and/or a summative evaluation of classmates' work

Objective: To conduct peer evaluation to improve student work, build community through peer evaluation, and assist the instructor in evaluation of student work

Author: Thomas J. C. Smyth, PhD, University of South Carolina Aiken, smyth@usca.edu

Instructions

Showing work to others increases the probability that any strengths and weaknesses will be identified. Conduct an evaluation of your classmate's work using the rubric at this URL *[to be inserted by the instructor]*. This is a Google form that you will complete online and that will generate a spreadsheet of responses. The instructor will share the results with you anonymously following the due date. You then may use the evaluation to modify your work as you think appropriate based upon the peer evaluations.

Instructions for the Instructor

Construct an evaluation rubric for an assignment. Enter the details of the rubric on a Google form at Google Docs. Post the URL for the Google form for your students. Once students have completed their evaluations, view the resulting spreadsheet. Organize the spreadsheet as appropriate (by alphabetizing names and deleting columns, for example) and then post it as a web page for students to review and use.

Activity Author's Note

I have used this technique in several courses with a variety of assignments. Students have been frank in their peer reviews and have found the feedback to be extremely useful. This technique has resulted in improved quality of student work.

The activity supports two of the National Standards for Online Teaching (NACOL): "[Instructor] creates opportunities for self-reflection or assessment . . . within the online environment (e.g., classroom assessment techniques, teacher evaluations, teacher peer reviews)" and "The teacher demonstrates frequent and effective strategies that enable both teacher and students to complete self- and pre-assessments."

Book Authors' Note

This type of peer assessment works best when the learners remain anonymous and a safe environment has been established for the learning community. It is also beneficial to be able to align any activity with national, state, or local standards.

ONLINE ROLE-PLAY

Task: Multiweek scaffolded activity that leads up to a conference on a complex and debated contemporary issue

Objective: To guide knowledge attainment about a contemporary world problem so that students can study, understand, and represent one of the included perspectives

Author: Michelle Rogers-Estable, EdS, University of the People, mre @michelleestable.com

Instructions

Students are assigned to a group of three or four fellow students and given a country in the Middle East that they are to represent. Each week up to the final week of the course, students are assigned exercises concerning the week's topics, in order to build up their expertise and knowledge about that country and the issues in that region.

For example:

- In week 1, students will study and analyze the main people involved in the politics and contemporary debates, and then they choose a figure from that country, region, or area to represent (such as the prime minister, president, or a delegate).

- In week 2, they research the country to learn more about its demographics, religion(s), and history.

- In week 3, they begin researching the issues and conflicts, such as the water crisis or border disputes.

- An additional topic is assigned each of the following weeks until the final week's concluding conference.

- Students complete work each week to prepare them for the final week of the course, during which the instructor hosts the United Nations' Peace Conference—an online forum that all students will participate in concerning specific Middle East concerns.

- The instructor participates in the culminating conference as the UN conference chairperson.

Activity Author's Notes

In this scenario a study of political issues in the Middle East was used. But that topic can be exchanged for any debated contemporary issue. The goal of the role-play is to study a topic deeply and then discuss the issues with others in the class in the conference during the last week of their study. This activity can be used for any topic that has highly disputed themes, such as climate change, preservation of cultural traditions, reintroduction of wolves to Yellowstone National Park, land use policy, or drilling for oil. I have used it in an environmental science course concerning climate change and also in a diversity studies course concerning problems in the Middle East.

It is best if students are first asked what their own political views are before being assigned to a group, and then are purposely put into the opposing group. For example, if they side with Israel's increased use of water from the Jordan River, they might be assigned to represent Palestine or one of the other countries that hold the opposing view that Israel is depleting the river. Or, if they side with the reintroduction of wolves into Yellowstone Park, then they would be put into the ranchers group that opposes it. Alternatively, if they agree with the research on climate change, they might be put into the group of business owners who are worried about policy that affects economic growth.

To the extent possible, place students in a group that holds the opposite view they had upon entering the course. The main point of this exercise is not only to learn about the complexity of different perspectives on important issues, but to help them learn about and understand new perspectives and angles they did not previously see. They cannot do this if they end up representing the views they already held when they entered the course.

This activity was used in twelve different Diversity Studies classes over the course of a year. The feedback was positive. Students said that the scaffolding of knowledge each week allowed them to build up their knowledge about one topic and to feel they could expertly discuss the conflict topics in the Middle East. Most important, several students each course said that through this process they understood for the first time why the problems in the Middle East were so difficult to work out and why people there were so passionate about them. They said it really opened their eyes to the complexity of the situation.

Online learning examples. In the online asynchronous discussion forum, the students found pictures of their personas to put in their posts and used that person's name. In distance learning situations, this kind of exercise works very well in a virtual world situation such as SecondLife, in which students can create avatars of their personas. It is also possible to host the conference via Twitter and social media sites that allow for interaction among the students through their smartphones and other Internet devices.

Book Authors' Note

Weekly topics can be chosen by the instructor with the learning goal of providing each student with a more in-depth understanding of the assigned country and its challenges. The final conference can be held face-to-face or online through a chat or interactive broadcast. When a visual medium is possible, it enhances the experience when students dress in costumes for the event. I held a debate in one course based on learning theories. The behaviorist dressed in a lab coat and brought a live rat to the class. The situated cognition folks wore costumes resembling amoebas. The constructivist wore tie-dyed shirts and beads to represent 1960s free-spirited hippies. The behaviorist even brought a cake with icing that stated: I drool for Pavlov.

VIRTUAL DINING MEETING

Task: To determine virtual menu items for a meeting or group discussion

Objective: To set the stage for an introductory discussion for a virtual meeting

Author: Paula Dawidowicz, PhD, Walden University, paula.dawidowicz@waldenu.edu

Instructions

A fun way to plan your team facilitation activity—or to hold any team meeting, for that matter—is to incorporate a virtual dining experience. The discussions facilitator needs to choose a restaurant that has online menus available. It is important to include the restaurant's web link in the invitation to the call along with the agenda for the meeting. Here's an example of a recent communication:

> In the spirit of graduation this month, we'll meet virtually in Minneapolis's Dakota Jazz Club and Restaurant (the best of the North and the South merged). To get an idea of your virtual food options (boy, are the calories better this way!), here's the web address: http://www.dakotacooks.com/food-wine-spirits/menus.

Book Authors' Note

The challenge of this task is to find a broad range of menus from which to choose. Paris, New York City, or Cleveland are all possible locations. I personally am a fan of diners, drive-ins, and dives, so my choices may be very different from yours. Dr. MaryFriend Shepard of Walden University offers a variation of this activity: she has her students all go to the same brand of café or restaurant in different cities and then enter the chat room using the available Wi-Fi. Starbucks is her favorite to date.

Phase 5 Activities: Continue

Learner empowerment and the realization of a transformational learning experience are the ultimate goals for the final phase in the Phases of Engagement model. The reflective portion of this phase allows students to see how far they have journeyed since the beginning of the course. The application of the content knowledge in the community allows for a validation of the learning experience and students' newly enhanced skills. The combination of reflection and application as the cornerstones of Phase 5 activities result in students engaged not only with their own knowledge acquisition but with their fellow learning community and the global community. Table 9.1 lists elements to consider when designing a Phase 5 activity. Table 9.2 lists the activities contained in this chapter.

Table 9.1. Checklist for an Effective Phase 5 Activity

	Yes	No	Comments
1. Does the activity ask for a synthesis of the learning experience?			
2. Does it require the learner to share his or her experiences?			
3. Does it allow for honest and open responses?			
4. Does it require a person to draw a conclusion regarding how he or she has changed over the course of the learning experience?			
5. Is the activity insightful and nonthreatening?			

Source: Adapted from *Engaging the Online Learner: Activities and Resources for Creative Instruction,* by R. M. Conrad and J. A. Donaldson, 2004, 2011, Jossey-Bass.

Table 9.2. Phase 5 Activities to Try

Activity	Type	Purpose
Cloud Quilt	Group reflection using Wordle	To summarize core concepts in a collaborative shared document with subsequent reflections using Wordle
Concept Quilt	Visual reflection	To creatively share important key points in a visual format
Dollar Store	Reflective sharing	To identify and share important key points
Do Over	Reflective sharing	To determine how to improve engagement in the next learning opportunity
Job Interview	Reflective sharing	To discuss how this learning experience will be incorporated into their career
Lessons Learned	Reflective group discussion	To pinpoint and share key points based on five questions
Lessons Meet Application	Application of course concepts	To recognize opportunities for application of course concepts
Poem from the Mind of . . .	Application of concepts for a specific content area	To help students gain empathy for individuals who suffer from mental health disorders
Poetry Meets Theory	Reflection on concepts through poetry	To enforce students' basic understanding of a new concept or theory in a creative way
Show Me the Money	Application implementation within the community	To identify and implement key points from the perspective of application
Talk with Grandmother	Reflective task to articulate key concepts	To discover and concisely articulate key points
Virtual Door	Reflection on advances in content learning	To distinguish and share individual and group advances in content learning

CLOUD QUILT

Task: Student-driven generation of course content across the semester using a shared doc, Wordle, and a common publishing area

Objective: To summarize core concepts in a collaborative shared document with subsequent reflections on the Wordle as a snapshot of diverse inputs

Author: Kathleen Gradel, EdD, professor, SUNY Fredonia, gradel@fredonia.edu

Instructions for Students

1. Read or review assigned course materials.

2. Post to a shared doc the words or phrases that come to mind relating to the reading(s) or material(s).

3. After everyone has posted, copy all or a subset of the terms into a Wordle (http://www.wordle.net). Format as you wish. Note that the more frequently a term is used, the larger it appears in the image.

4. Make a screenshot or screen capture of your final word cloud.

5. Insert your image on the course's "word cloud quilt," ensuring that you have signed your posting.

6. Go to the course wiki and comment on your review of one or more of the final word clouds in terms of their capturing key concepts or reactions to the article(s) and materials reviewed.

Instructions for the Instructor

1. Prep the materials to be reviewed, posting them as needed.

2. Decide on the word cloud tool to use (such as Wordle, TagCloud, Wordsift, or Tagul) and gather tutorial information on its use.

3. Build a shared doc for students to use. I currently use Google Docs and have used ZohoWriter (https://writer.zoho.com/home?serviceurl=%2Findex.do) or iEtherpad (http://ietherpad.com) at times. There are almost endless options out there.

4. Prepare a posting venue on your learning management system, wiki, or blog for students to (a) post their word cloud images and (b) engage in a final discussion based on their review of the entire group of word clouds.

5. Provide links to tutorials for students to gear up to the tech demands of the task.

6. Post directions for the assignment.

7. "Shadow" the process, monitoring their posts; guide students in timing, accuracy, and the like as needed.

8. Identify and clarify for students how this work factors into the grading system.

Activity Author's Note

Asking students to do this helps them reinforce their understanding of concepts in readings and pay attention to others' contributions. It also taps into students' diverse learning preferences and styles. Many love the "bling" that they have produced!

I have used various media for this; instructors will want to choose the publishing platform(s) according to one or more of these variables: (a) reinforcing other tech use in the course and/or (b) extending students' use of technology tools and/or (c) the highest comfort level for the instructor to facilitate.

Examples are helpful in prompting good work. It is important to value this work in the grading framework, since this is a way to track students' formative use of at least some of the course's readings and media.

Don't overdo it. ☺

Book Authors' Note

Students and faculty both enjoy incorporating word clouds into the course to visually represent the key concepts learned. Consider asking students to each submit their list of words and then create one word cloud to state the collective image of the concept. This approach is also effective for written papers, since the key words are highlighted in the final image. It helps a student to determine emerging themes in research.

CONCEPT QUILT

Task: To reflect upon the key course concepts in a visual format

Objective: To share important points of content

Author: J. Ana Donaldson, EdD, online educator and consultant, ana
.donaldson@cfu.net

Instructions

The process of learning has been compared to the creation of a quilt. Everyone brings their own perceptions and experiences to the experience. Each new idea, concept, or revelation brings a new color or texture to the activity and completed project. It is important to remember that the final learning experience will differ for each individual and for each class. You will be asked to share your own interpretation of our class experience related to a given topic. Your task is to provide a graphic representation of an assigned concept. You may use a graphic design software program or use the drawing tools within Word to create your image. The final image needs to be three inches wide by five inches high. You will need to provide a 250-word written description of your image. Your image needs to align with your written description. You will also need to respond to at least two other students' graphic images.

Activity Author's Note

It is critical that the digital quilt is actually put together. You can complete this task yourself or offer extra credit to a student with web design skills. The size of the quilt will be determined by the number of submissions. Most quilts work best as four squares by six squares. With larger classes, I've also designed this as a group task per concept. I always include one or two blocks in the center for the course identifying information and the class member names. It is great if you can have each of the images linked to the student-provided explanation. A rollover feature is also beneficial for this additional information. Another design feature is to use thick colored lines for the quilt block to tie everything together. If the class meets for a final face-to-face session, you can expand this activity to have each class member or group create the actual image on a three-by-five-inch felt square. You can then use hot glue to place each square on a prepared piece of cloth where the squares are defined by glued-down ribbons. The square can be glued as the individual reads their explanation. This activity can be a very powerful final reflective moment for the class members.

DOLLAR STORE

Task: To define and reflect upon the course or topic concepts

Objective: To identify and share important key points

Author: J. Ana Donaldson, EdD, online educator and consultant, ana
.donaldson@cfu.net

Instructions

Over the course of the class, we have introduced many concepts and ideas. Our discussions have explored a variety of topics. They have been focused on using words primarily to share our thoughts. For this activity, you are being challenged to express a key concept in a visual way. Your task is to go to a local variety store and find an object that expresses a key concept discussed in class. You are limited to spending one dollar on this object. You then will need to submit a picture of your object along with a 250-word description explaining why you chose this object. Include in your discussion how your understanding or awareness of this concept may have evolved during the course of the class. Include in your discussion whether you think your final object would be the same one you might have chosen at the beginning of the course. Which of the lessons you've learned will you carry into future learning opportunities?

Activity Author's Note

This task causes the students to reflect on the concepts discussed during the course and then choose one of importance to them. A montage can be created of the final objects. I've used a graphic of a quilt to display the results of this activity. Refer to the preceding Concept Quilt activity for an example.

DO OVER

Task: Reflect on how well students engaged in the course

Objective: To determine ways in which engagement can be utilized and improved in future learning situations

Author: Rita-Marie Conrad, PhD, Institute for Educational Excellence, Duke University School of Nursing, ritamarie.conrad@duke.edu

Instructions

In addition to learning content and developing knowledge in this course, another goal has been to help you cultivate your skills as a collaborator and a self-directed learner. Take a moment to reflect on these questions:

- In what ways do you feel more confident in participating in team learning activities?
- In what ways do you still need to grow as a team member?
- How can you be a better collaborator as you move on to other courses and learning experiences?

Activity Author's Note

The product of this activity also informs the instructor as to whether the Phases of Engagement were successful, so be sure to reflect on the results and see how the engagement experience and activities might be fine-tuned.

JOB INTERVIEW

Task: Using the reverse-brainstorming strategy, analyze how your teamwork should function

Objective: To develop a team contract or improve teamwork

Author: Rita-Marie Conrad, PhD, Institute for Educational Excellence, Duke University School of Nursing, ritamarie.conrad@duke.edu

Instructions

You are being interviewed for a promotion. Write at least a half-page response to this question: How did taking this course prepare you for this promotion?

Activity Author's Note

This activity can also be paired with the Dream Job icebreaker in Chapter 5. Learners can be asked to refer back to that dream job activity and write a cover letter for it discussing how this course prepared them for the job.

LESSONS LEARNED

Task: To define and reflect upon the course or topic concepts

Objective: To identify and share important key points based on five questions

Author: J. Ana Donaldson, EdD, online educator and consultant, ana .donaldson@cfu.net

Instructions

During our shared learning experience this semester, many concepts were introduced and discussed. It is time to reflect on what this has meant to you personally and how you will take these lessons beyond this class. Post to the discussion thread your responses to these five questions:

1. What new concepts or ideas did you learn in this course?

2. What are the major concepts?

3. What examples can you cite to support what you believe are the major concepts?

4. What questions do you still have?

5. How will you apply the concepts learned in future opportunities?

Activity Author's Note

This activity borrows heavily on the Focused Listening activity in Chapter 6. Students are asked to synthesize the course content and then share their own learning experience with others. It also provides the critical "So what" moment—now that learning has occurred, how will it be transferred to subsequent learning opportunities or applications?

LESSONS MEET APPLICATION

Task: To reflect upon the course and identify authentic applications

Objective: To identify opportunities for application of course concepts

Author: J. Ana Donaldson, EdD, online educator and consultant, ana .donaldson@cfu.net

Instructions

During the course of the semester, many new concepts have been identified and discussed. Think about which key concepts you might apply in your community to make a difference. List the ideas that could have a social impact. Then identify an agency in your community where this concept could be implemented. Include a description of how you would implement this concept in that community organization.

One example might be the concept of social networking. The agency chosen is a nonprofit organization that works with senior citizens. The application is the use of Skype for seniors to stay in contact with grandchildren. The description includes how this information is delivered to the seniors. Don't forget to include how the results of the delivery of the information will be assessed to evaluate the seniors' learning experience.

Activity Author's Note

This is an example of theory meeting practice. The application of learned concepts empowers students to become transformative learners and agents for change. The lessons learned in the class become authentic when applied to community needs. This activity becomes powerful when the students follow through and actually work with the agency to implement the changes. As the instructor, you can assist the students by providing a list of key concepts learned and resources for identifying community agencies.

POEM FROM THE MIND OF . . .

Task: Writing a poem from the mind or view of an individual suffering from a mental illness (or other condition)

Objective: To help students gain empathy for individuals who suffer from mental health disorders

Author: Meredith Brown, MS, Piedmont Technical College, brown.md@ptc.edu

Instructions for Students

Students are asked to choose a mental health disorder from a list of disorders provided. They are instructed to choose a disorder that they have little or no experience with, not to select disorders they or someone they know has been diagnosed with, and to use their textbook and approved sources to learn more about the disorder. After they have investigated their chosen disorder, they are to write a poem from the mind of someone who is diagnosed with the disorder. The poem can be filmed by webcam, or students can use other media such as Animoto (movie maker) or PowerPoint to express their poem. A live chat time is set up for individuals who have questions about the assignment or would like information on how to make PowerPoint presentations or videos. After completion, students are asked to post their creations in the discussion board area called "Poems." Students are asked to reply respectfully to each others' poems. Poems can be posted anonymously, but students must send the title of their poem to the instructor via e-mail for grading. After the assignment is complete, students are to post what they thought about the assignment in a separate discussion.

Instructions for the Instructor

Instructors should set up a resource page with links to free software or websites that students can use to make their videos. In addition, there are tutorials on YouTube that teach students how to make narrated PowerPoint presentations. Instructors should carefully monitor posts and replies from students. If the student expresses the essence of the mental disorder, they receive a pass on the assignment. It is difficult to grade creativity and how individuals express themselves, so instruct the students to be creative and rest assured that as long as they don't misrepresent the mental health disorder, they will earn a pass on the assignment. The additional postings with their thoughts about the assignment are not graded, but are strongly encouraged.

Activity Author's Note

The feedback from students on this activity has been amazing. Students report "not understanding what schizophrenia really was" before they began. They say the activity helped them to see mental illness as a real sickness, rather than something a person needs to get over. Students also report discovering it is not the fault of the person with the disorder, once students really think about what the affected individual is going through. This is a sensitive topic, but one that is too often brushed aside in general psychology. This is an effective way for students to gain a deeper understanding of mental illness and share it in a way that is safe and creative. This activity can be applied to many other subjects. An English instructor might assign a Poem from the Mind of a famous author, and a political science or history instructor might assign a Poem from the Mind of a political figure. There are many possible applications, and this assignment allows students to think critically and share their creativity, a quality that is sometimes neglected in online courses. I have uploaded two videos of this activity so that readers can view them: http://www.youtube.com/watch?v=3WzRWPz84J4 and http://www.youtube.com/watch?v=PreS_fi43hk&feature=related.

Book Authors' Note

As the activity author states, this activity can be used in so many instances to gain further understanding of the subjects presented in class. Additional ideas include a poem from someone coping with a terminal disease, learning about Piaget's theories, an individual writing home from the warfront, or any prompt that asks a student to take a view on a topic from a personal perspective.

POETRY MEETS THEORY

Task: To be done at the end of an introduction of a new concept or theory or end of a unit

Objective: To enforce students' basic understanding of a new concept or theory in a creative way

Author: J. Ana Donaldson, EdD, online educator and consultant, ana .donaldson@cfu.net

Instructions

Working with your partner(s), you will need to describe the components of the provided theory or concept by using the cinquain poetic form as your format. There are five components to the cinquain poetic form:

Two words

Three words

Four words

Five words

Two words

Your group will need to determine the five key components of the theory or concept. Using the cinquain format, assign the key components in order from 1 through 5. Then assign the number of words required for each of the five components. You may not use the components as part of your chosen poetry.

Example. Using the Seels and Richey (1994) definition of the evaluation subdomains, describe making a peanut butter and jelly sandwich.

Subdomain	Cinquain Format	Making a PB&J Sandwich
Problem analysis	Two words (theme, problem, or object)	Mystery food
Criterion-referenced measurement	Three words (criteria)	Gooey creamy sweet
Formative evaluation	Four words (process or activity)	Spreading to edges evenly
Summative evaluation	Five words (final result)	Tasty crushed nuts, smashed fruit
Conclusion	Two words	Childhood memory

Post your completed poem with an explanation of why your group chose the specific subtopics. Include what you learned from this activity that clarified your understanding of the theory and its components.

Activity Author's Note

This exercise is a creative way to have students review complex theories or concepts from a new perspective. It is a great vehicle for collaborative discussion and interaction. The key to developing this concept-specific activity is to find a topic that can be divided into four or five elements with a final conclusion.

SHOW ME THE MONEY

Task: To describe key concepts and identify the application of the course content

Objective: To identify and implement key points from the perspective of application

Author: J. Ana Donaldson, EdD, online educator and consultant, ana .donaldson@cfu.net

Instructions

The task is to take the lessons learned into the community to identify ways to implement the concepts learned. The first step of the process is to describe the key concepts learned during the class. Identify and discuss the concepts that have the potential for social impact. Explain the possible instructional strategies that might be used to present these concepts. List at least three community organizations that might implement this concept, and give an overview of each organization. Choose one organization from your list for concept implementation. Then find a grant that matches the application and the organization's needs. Research current requests for proposals and find a possible grant match. Provide a final discussion of the lessons learned through this process. Post your documentation to the assigned dropbox.

Outline of Documentation

- Key concepts
- Social impact
- Instructional strategies suggested
- Community organizations

    Historical background

    Mission or vision

    Target audience

    Current programs

    Identified needs

- Explanation of chosen organization

- Grant request for proposal
- Proposed budget for the project
- Summary

Activity Author's Note

The intent of this activity is to make the lessons learned in the class transfer to the community. Learning is about what happens after the class ends. As the instructor, you will need to provide a level of scaffolding for your students. Providing grant resources will be helpful to students, as will listings of local community organizations. One resource that I've found helpful is *Grant Writing for Dummies* (Browning, 2008). Ultimately, the final documentation might also be shared with the selected community organization.

TALK WITH GRANDMOTHER

Task: To define and reflect upon the course or topic concepts

Objective: To identify and concisely articulate important key points

Author: J. Ana Donaldson, EdD, online educator and consultant, ana .donaldson@cfu.net

Instructions

During the course of this class, you have explored many new concepts and ideas. One of the ways you can show that you have learned this material is by putting this newly gained knowledge into your own words. Your task is to explain to your grandmother or another family member what you learned in the course and how that is important to your profession. You will be asked to audiotape or videotape your discussion. A completed transcript of the conversation will be required along with a digital copy of the audio or video file. The basic guidelines are as follows:

- The discussion should be limited to ten to fifteen minutes.
- It needs to include at least three concepts presented during the course.
- You will need to describe how this course will affect you as a practitioner.
- Questions or comments from your grandmother.
- Final thoughts on the interview session and class.

Activity Author's Note

This task builds upon the notion that "sometimes we learn more when we teach." When students put course concepts into their own words, it encourages student ownership of the concepts. Explaining how this course is relevant to real-world situations is also a key component.

VIRTUAL DOOR

Task: To define and reflect upon the course or topic concepts

Objective: To identify and share individual and group advances in content learning

Author: J. Ana Donaldson, EdD, online educator and consultant, ana .donaldson@cfu.net

Instructions

Think about the first day of class for this course. Then think about your current state of understanding about the course content and future concept applications. The objective for this course experience was for you to walk through a door into a new room of knowledge. You are asked to document your understandings before and after you learn key concepts. A beginning place for this task is the learning objectives given on the course syllabus. List the course objectives, and for each one describe your initial understandings followed by your current level of knowledge. Include a description of the importance of each objective to your professional world and possible authentic applications of the newly acquired information.

Activity Author's Note

This activity functions as a summative self-evaluation of the student's attainment of the course objectives. It also provides the Phase 5 additional link to how the information can be transferred to authentic applications. Extra credit can be offered for those students who wish to go the extra mile and show how they have aligned their specific learning experiences with local, state, or national professional standards.

References

Aldrich, C. (2009). *Learning online with games, simulations, and virtual worlds*. San Francisco: Jossey-Bass.

Attewell, J. (2005). *Mobile technologies and learning: A technology update and m-learning project summary*. UK: Learning and Skills Development Agency.

Barbour, M. (n.d.). *Strategies for students and instructors how to improve online groupwork*. Retrieved April 20, 2011, from http://www.michaelbarbour.com/research/pubs/el08-koh.pdf.

Barkley, E. F. (2010). *Student engagement techniques: A handbook for college faculty*. San Francisco: Jossey-Bass.

Boettcher, J. V., & Conrad, R. M. (2010). *The online teaching survival guide: Simple and practical pedagogical tips*. San Francisco: Jossey-Bass.

Bonk, C. (2007, October 5). TravelinEdMan blog entry. Retrieved May 1, 2010, from http://travelinedman.blogspot.com/2007_10_01_archive.html.

Bonk, C., & Zhang, K. (2008). *Empowering online learning: 100+ activities for reading, reflecting, displaying and doing*. San Francisco: Jossey-Bass.

Brookfield, S. D. (1995). *Becoming a critically reflective teacher*. San Francisco: Jossey-Bass.

Browning, B. (2008). *Grant writing for dummies*, 3rd ed. Hoboken, NJ: Wiley.

Bruner, J. (1966). *Toward a theory of instruction*. Cambridge, MA: Harvard University Press.

Cavanaugh, C. (2009). Research committee issues brief: Examining communication and interaction in online teaching. Retrieved April 30, 2010, from http://www.inacol.org/research/docs/NACOL_QualityTeaching-lr.pdf.

Cercone, K. (2008). Characteristics of adult learners with implications for online learning design. *AACE Journal, 16*(2), 137–159.

Coates, J. (2007). *Generational learning styles*. River Falls, WI: LERN Books.

Conceicao, S.C.O., & Lehman, R. M. (2011). *Managing online instructor workload: Strategies for finding balance and success*. San Francisco: Jossey-Bass.

Conrad, R. M., & Donaldson, J. A. (2004). *Engaging the online learner: Activities and resources for creative instruction*. San Francisco: Jossey-Bass.

Conrad, R. M., & Donaldson, J. A. (2011). *Engaging the online learner: Activities and resources for creative instruction* (2nd ed.). San Francisco: Jossey-Bass.

Coombs, N. (2010). *Making online teaching accessible: Inclusive course design for students with disabilities.* San Francisco: Jossey-Bass.

Dewey, J. (1997). *Democracy and education: An introduction to the philosophy of education.* New York: Free Press. (Original work published 1916)

Draves, W. A., & Coates, J. (2011). *The pedagogy of the 21st century.* River Falls, WI: LERN Books.

Eisenberger, J., Conti-D'Antonio, M., & Bertrando, R. (2005). *Self-efficacy: Raising the bar for all students* (2nd ed.). Larchmont, NY: Eye on Education.

Finkelstein, J. (2006). *Learning in real time: Synchronous teaching and learning online.* San Francisco: Jossey-Bass.

Garrison, D. R., & Cleveland-Innes, M. (2005). Facilitating cognitive presence in online learning: Interaction is not enough. *The American Journal of Distance Education, 19*(3), 133–248.

Herring, M. C., & Smaldino, S. E. (2005). *Planning for interactive distance education: A handbook.* Washington, DC: Association for Educational Communication and Technology.

Houle, C. (1988). *The inquiring mind* (2nd ed.). Madison: University of Wisconsin.

Knowles, M. S. (1980). *The modern practice of adult education: From pedagogy to andragogy.* Englewood Cliffs: Prentice Hall/Cambridge.

Kop, R., & Hill, A. (2008). Connectivism: Learning theory of the future or vestige of the past? *The International Review of Research in Open and Distance Learning, 9*(3). Retrieved April 20, 2011, from http://www.irrodl.org/index.php/irrodl/article/view /523/1103.

Lehman, R. M., & Conceicao, S.C.O. (2010). *Creating a sense of presence in online teaching: How to "be there" for distance learners.* San Francisco: Jossey-Bass.

Merriam, S. B., Caffarella, R. S., & Baumgartner, L. M. (2007). *Learning in adulthood: A comprehensive guide* (3rd ed.). San Francisco: Jossey-Bass.

Mezirow, J., & Associates. (2000). *Learning as transformation: Critical perspectives on a theory in progress.* San Francisco: Jossey-Bass.

Munro, J. S. (1998). *Presence at a distance: The educator-learner relationship in distance learning.* ASCDE Research Monograph 16. University Park: Pennsylvania State University.

National Education Technology Plan (2010). *Transforming American education: Learning powered by technology.* Washington, DC: U.S. Department of Education.

Oosterhof, A., Conrad, R. M., & Ely, D. P. (2008). *Assessing learners online.* Upper Saddle River: Pearson.

Palloff, R., & Pratt, K. (2005). *Collaborating online: Learning together in community.* San Francisco: Jossey-Bass.

Palloff, R. M., & Pratt, K. (2007). *Building online learning communities: Effective strategies for the virtual student classroom.* San Francisco: Jossey-Bass.

Palloff, R. M., & Pratt, K. (2011). *The excellent online instructor: Strategies for professional development.* San Francisco: Jossey-Bass.

Parra, J. (2011). Technology & collaborative learning: Scaffolding for student success. Paper presented at Sloan-C 4th Annual International Symposium, July 2011. Retrieved April 20, 2011, from http://sloanconsortium.org/conferences/2011/et4online/technology-collaborative-learning-scaffolding-student-success.

Piaget, J. (1969). *The mechanisms of perception.* London: Routledge & Kegan Paul.

Quinn, C. N. (2012). *The mobile academy: mLearning for higher education.* San Francisco: Jossey-Bass.

Schellens, T., & Valcke, M. (2006). Fostering knowledge construction in university students through asynchronous discussion groups [Electronic version]. *Computers & Education, 46,* 349–370.

Seels, B., & Richey, R. (1994). *Instructional technology: The definition and domains of the field.* Washington, DC: Association for Educational Communications and Technology.

Shank, P. (2007). *The online learning idea book: 95 proven ways to enhance technology-based and blended learning.* San Francisco: Jossey-Bass.

Siemens, G. (2006). *Knowing knowledge.* Retrieved from http://www.Lulu.com.

Siemens, G. (2008, January 27). *Learning and knowing in networks: Changing roles for educators and designers.* Paper presented to ITFORUM. Retrieved May 1, 2010, from http://it.coe.uga.edu/itforum/Paper105/Siemens.pdf.

Smith, R. M. (2008). *Conquering the content: A step-by-step guide to online course design.* San Francisco: Jossey-Bass.

Soloway, E., Grant, W., Tinker, R., Roschelle, J., Mills, M., Resnick, M., Berg, R., & Eisenberg, M. (1999). Science in the palms of their hands. *Communications of the Associations for Computing Machinery, 42,* 8.

Vygotsky, L. S. (1978). *Mind in society: The development of higher psychological processes.* Cambridge, MA: Harvard University Press.

Wagner, E. (2008). Mainstreaming mobile learning. *Learning Solutions Magazine,* pp. 1–3. Retrieved April 20, 2011, from http://www.learningsolutionsmag.com/articles/92/mainstreaming-mobile-learning/print.

Watkins, R. (2005). *75 e-Learning activities: Making online learning interactive.* San Francisco: Jossey-Bass.

West, J., & West, M. (2009). *Using wikis for online collaboration*: The power of the read-write we. San Francisco: Jossey-Bass.

Wexler, S., Schlenker, B., Brown, J., Metcalf, D., Quinn, C., Thor, E. Van Barneveld, A., & Wagner, E. (2007). *360 research report mobile learning: What it is, why it matters, and how to incorporate it into your learning strategy.* Santa Rosa, CA: eLearning Guild.

Index

grading, 40–46; and issues paper rubric, 41–44; and peer evaluation form, 45; and phase-based assessment, 47; and providing feedback, 46; use of technology for, 46–47; and using assessment to improve engagement, 47–49

Online engagement: and creating sense of presence, 11–12; and engaged educator, 10; and engagement in today's online learning environment, 6–7; and foundations of engagement, 4–6; and impact of social networking and connectivism, 7–8; and increasing transformational learning, 8–9; instructor's role and philosophy in, 10–11; and mobile technology, 12–13; process of, 6; state of, 3–13; and twenty-first-century learner, 9

Online Learner: Resources and Strategies for Faculty (Palloff and Pratt), 100

Online Resource Time Travel (Phase 2 activity), 75, 83–84

Online Role-Play (Phase 4 activity), 116, 126–128

Oosterhof, A., 38, 39

P

Palestine, 127

Pallof, R., 3, 24

Parra, J., 15

Passion (Phase 1 activity), 55, 67

Pavlov, I., 128

Pearson (Ning sponsor), 104

Peer evaluation form, 45

Phase-based assessment, 47

Phases of Engagement, 7, 16; appropriate activities for, 20–22; evolution of, 14–23; and Phase 1: connect, 15–17; and Phase 2: communicate, 17–18; and Phase 3: collaborate, 19–20; and Phase 4: co-facilitate, 19–20; and Phase 5: continue, 20; summary, 22–23

Phases of Engagement, implementing, 24–35; and changing course, 32–33; and dealing with difficult students, 34; and engaged course planning tool, 27; and engaging large classes, 26–28; and instructor time management, 31–32; and managing engagement, 28–29; and "online educator's Bill of Rights," 33–34; and question of online or blended, 25–26; and timely communication, 29–30

Piaget, J., 4, 5, 142

Piedmont Technical College, 141

Poem from the Mind of... (Phase 5 activity), 132, 141–142

Poetry Meets Theory (Phase 5 activity), 132, 143–144

PowerPoint (Microsoft), 21, 46, 141

Pratt, K., 3, 24

Presence, creating sense of, 11–12

Q

Quinn, C. N., 12

QWERTY keyboard, 96–98

R

Rainbow (Phase 1 activity), 55, 68–69

Reading a Brief (Phase 2 activity), 75, 85–86

Reincarnation (Phase 2 activity), 75, 87